Hazelnuts and Moorhens' Eggs

Recollections of a Childhood Spent in the Wiltshire Countryside, 1940–1955

Hazelnuts and Moorhens' Eggs
Recollections of a Childhood Spent in the Wiltshire Countryside, 1940–1955

Rod Broomham

ATHENA PRESS
LONDON

Hazelnuts and Moorhens' Eggs
*Recollections of a Childhood Spent in the
Wiltshire Countryside, 1940–1955*
Copyright © Rod Broomham 2009

All Rights Reserved

No part of this book may be reproduced in any form
by photocopying or by any electronic or mechanical means,
including information storage or retrieval systems,
without permission in writing from both the copyright
owner and the publisher of this book.

ISBN 978 1 84748 606 6

First published 2009 by
ATHENA PRESS
Queen's House, 2 Holly Road
Twickenham TW1 4EG
United Kingdom

Printed for Athena Press

Food for the Table

I was seven years of age and bursting with pride as I dashed into the cottage and presented my mum with her first, and what was to be her last, oven-ready blackbird.

Weeks of stalking the hedgerows on my journeys to and from school, with my catapult at the ready, had finally paid off. A plump blackbird had at last fallen prey to 'Young Jim', hunter-gatherer. The priority now was to prepare the bird; this could be done during my mile-and-a-half walk home from the village school. With the dexterous use of my penknife and the probing of nimble fingers the entrails were removed; clouds of plucked feathers accompanied me to within a few yards of the little thatched cottage that was home.

The reception wasn't quite what I had expected; Mum's flashing blue eyes and gasp of horror, followed swiftly by the application of her hand to my left ear, was definitely the opposite reaction to the one my dad received when he presented food for the table. Perhaps my blackbird wasn't as big as the usual pheasant or duck that Dad brought home, but then, neither was I as big as Dad. What had caused this outburst? As on similar demonstrative occasions I took refuge in the outhouse. This always proved to be the most prudent course of action. It would give Mum time to reflect and, hopefully, appreciate my contribution to the daily family fare.

The cottage was located in Manningford, a village composed of three regions, Manningford Abbots, Manningford Bruce and Manningford Bohune. We lived in the northern region, which was Abbots, referred to by some as Abbass. The cottage was very basic as were most dwellings in the villages of that era. They were known as 'tied' cottages because they were provided by the farmer, or landowner, for his labourers.

There were very few working-class families that would aspire to owning their own homes in those days; therefore, to be tied to

Hazelnuts and Moorhens' Eggs

an employer in this way was a beneficial arrangement for both parties.

Our cottage was not of the 'chocolate box' variety that you will find on postcards and paintings that depict the idyllic village; very few of them were. The thatch was riddled with holes and protruding tufts of straw, created by nesting birds. Wire netting was not widely used to deter them as it is today. There was no thatcher's signature, – a straw pheasant for example, or the elaborate hazelwood latticework that make today's cottages look so attractive. Flowers did not have a place in a garden that was intended to provide food for the occupants of the dwelling. The 'chocolate box' cottage, to a great extent, was created by urban folk who moved into the country and bought and revamped the existing properties. In effect they have preserved the villages and, although Manningford today bears no resemblance to the village that I grew up in, it is now a pleasurable experience to wander down the country road and admire the greatly improved appearance of the cottages. Flowers have replaced vegetables in many gardens, while dwellings topped with thatched roofs are veritable works of art.

Our accommodation consisted of one room and a walk-in scullery on the ground floor, with two bedrooms above. An outhouse, or woodshed as it was also known, served as the equivalent of a utility room in latter-day parlance. We did not have electricity, main drainage or running water; oil lamps and candles provided lighting. The toilet was of the dry bucket type and the water was drawn from a well. The well sometimes ran dry in extremely hot spells and on such an occasion my brother and I, together with our neighbour's two daughters, would be sent to a nearby cattle trough.

The trough was situated in a nearby field and was served by an artesian well. This was never known to fail, and thankfully was always a reliable emergency supply for us. We would collect as much as we could carry in an assortment of containers, the average bucket being far too heavy, then it was back to the cottage, only to repeat the procedure until Mum was satisfied that we had collected enough for our daily needs. Many years later I recall being taken to a cattle trough for a school nature-study lesson and was amazed at the number of wild creatures that thrived in the water; mosquito larvae, water boatmen and strange spiders that ran across the water being among the wide variety of inhabitants. I can never remember Mum straining, or even boiling the water, so I assume that our emergency supply was either clear of wildlife or we ingested it! Heating and cooking facilities were provided by the black lead range, so named because it was kept in pristine condition by the frequent use of black lead polish. This was Mum's domain, or workstation, as Dad liked to call it. It was the centre of our little world. Mum would cook three meals a day, bake bread and pastries as well as heat her flat irons on the special trivet incorporated on the front of the fire basket. It was the family community centre. In the evenings we would gather round it, each member having a specified seat, mine being the outer shelf of the oven door. Today's events, and tomorrow's plans would be discussed until it was time for my brother and me to be escorted to our shared bedroom. Family bonding was fashioned and cemented around that range. The fact that there was only one room, shared by adults and children alike, prompts me to make a comparison to a warm and cosy bird's nest. There was always a pecking order in this nest, which had to be observed; this was most evident on bath night. The tin bath would be carried in and placed in front of the range where it was filled with hot water, heated in the copper.

Dad would be the first in. Once his ablutions were completed it would be Mum's turn, then it was my brother and me together. The water by this time had cooled quite considerably so we were not allowed to indulge in anything other than a quick scrubbing by Mum. I was not too disappointed as hygiene was not one of my finer points. If I wanted water play, the river Avon, or the many dykes and streams that abounded in my Wiltshire adventure park would provide plenty of opportunities.

Living in Manningford Abbots gave us the benefit of having the railway station, Manningford Halt, quite close to our cottage. Although we didn't travel by train the track provided us with a short cut to the nearby town of Pewsey, which was our nearest source of groceries and hardware. Mum would lead us along the edge of the track using the sleepers as stepping stones. I remember the ease

Hazelnuts and Moorhens' Eggs

with which she strode along, the spacing of the sleepers providing a regular pace for her that we could not equal. Our legs, being much shorter, made the journey far more difficult. Rail traffic was not heavy then and most adults did not regard using the track as a footpath a dangerous practice. In their defence, the noise of a steam engine huff puffing its way along the rails could be detected from a reasonable distance, allowing the pedestrian time to move to a safer position. An adult, with the safety of the children in their company being a priority, would not normally condone such an example of irresponsible behaviour, but the infrequency of public transport, as well as the cost, made it necessary. Many undertook the short cut in darkness, as the temptation of the Rex cinema in Pewsey became too great for those with a picture-going addiction to resist. For us young children, the cinema was beyond our aspirations; it would mean a move to the town and the acquisition of a few more years under our belts before we could experience the dark mysteries of 'the pictures'.

Manningford Abbots had its own church, hardly as big as our cottage in size. It was here that I was sent with my brother every Sunday to attend Sunday school. A book was provided and every attendance was recorded with a stamp, proof for Mum that we hadn't played hooky. The journey to the church was over fields and water meadows, another example of the shortest route being the most favoured; there was access by road but it was much further. In later years either my brother or I would visit the church to tend our grandparents' graves. The grounds were small but always tidy and well tended by the local population. On a recent visit to the area, after an absence of perhaps sixty years, I was disappointed to find that the church had been sold and the graveyard was completely overgrown. As I battled with the undergrowth trying to locate Gran and Granddad's graves, I realised that I had unconsciously started strolling down memory lane. My first recollection was of how we wandered almost anywhere without supervision, that we were free to play anywhere, and to a degree, with anything.

To reach this church as a child, using the route that we did, was no easy chore. We had to cross streams, avoid boggy ground, travel through fields of cattle and avoid becoming lacerated and impaled by barbed wire and fencing stakes. We achieved all of this, without getting covered in mud and grass stains, to arrive at Sunday school in a presentable manner. I realised that there are so many things that children today, through no fault of their own, are unable to take an active part in.

There is always the danger of looking back and viewing events through rose-coloured spectacles but, with hand on heart, I maintain that, despite the plethora of technology available to the children of today, my generation had the irreplaceable gift of the freedom to roam.

The Early Years

I was born in 1940 into what was soon to become an obligatory one-parent family. Obligatory insomuch that my father was called to serve with the Royal Marines in the conflict between Germany and Great Britain before I had learnt to walk or talk. Home was a village in the middle of the Wiltshire countryside; it was to provide me with my own adventure playground, a playground that would prove to be both recreational and educational. It supported a way of life that enabled a child to discover a wonderland of nature, presenting very few restrictions on one's freedom to roam.

I grew up quickly with many friends of similar ages and circumstances. My first clear memories are of joining the village school at the age of four. With my brother in charge, and my government-issue gas mask slung over my shoulder, we set out on the long journey to school. I remember being in complete awe of 'The Governess' who, on my arrival, divested me of my cardboard gas mask box; she placed it with others on a table at the back of the room before directing me to a desk and presenting me with a slate and stick of chalk. She was an expert in child psychology, for on my first day I was presented to the older class and awarded a round of applause for my drawing of a teapot. From that day forth school presented no problems for me. The school was a tiny building consisting of two classrooms. A glass-panelled door separated the infants from the older children. If an infant excelled at something, as I had with my chalk drawing, the dividing door was thrown open and the glowing child was rewarded with a round of applause from the older children. You catch more flies with honey than you do with vinegar! There was a small playground but, as the school was on the edge of a field, it was used only for assembly purposes and the occasional marking of a hopscotch complex.

We loved the village and its surrounding fields and streams.

All of our free time would be spent playing games and exploring. Due to the conflict between Germany and Great Britain most of the games we played were warlike in content. Water meadows became battlefields while a branch high in a tree became the cockpit of a Spitfire or Hurricane. I was usually a commando in the '1st Battalion', specialising in charges across water meadows, leaping ditches and producing the most blood-curdling shrieks a five-year-old is capable of. There were strange happenings that helped our adventures. For example, I remember one sunny day when the skies were suddenly filled with falling tinfoil strips; I assume that it was an experiment or some form of radar-blocking exercise but at the time it was both frightening and exciting. We wasted no time in collecting the foil strips from the fields and the surrounding hedges and fences. This material was added to our stock of come-in-handy-later bits and bobs. There were also many sightings of strange balloons at various times, meteorological perhaps; we never managed to find one of these, even though we would watch them descend into woodland areas. Manningford is not a great distance from Salisbury Plain where many military establishments abound. I suspect that this was the fount of the strange happenings witnessed by us at that time.

There were very few adult males in the village. Most had been conscripted to fight for king and country, which left the youngsters to the tender ministrations of the women. Perhaps I use the word 'tender' a little too loosely; my recollections of some of the ministrations were far from tender.

The names that we were christened with bore no resemblance to the names we were known by. My father's name was Jim; therefore I was known as 'Young Jim'. My brother was also Young Jim, and had there been more sons in the family they would also have been known as Young Jim. It was the village way to address all children by their fathers' names prefixed by 'young'. This applied only to the male members of the families; the girls were never addressed by their mothers' names. The system produced well-balanced females, but unfortunately quite a number of males suffering from identity crises.

Every adult, male or female, was an authority figure and had to be given obedience and respect. It worked well as I recall.

'Children's rights' did not hamper the upbringing of our generation. An African friend was talking to me recently and he told me that in his country they have a wise saying: 'It takes a whole village to raise a boy'. This was the case in my village. Every adult could correct or admonish you if you were found to be overstepping the boundaries of acceptable behaviour. The same adult would also ensure your safety and well-being, offering as much protection and guidance as your biological parents. No adult would allow children to endanger themselves or others if they were aware of a situation developing. My misdeeds, whenever possible, were committed out of sight of any figure of authority, thereby ensuring that they were often unaware.

As with all adventures and boyhood activities there will always be the occasional accident. It soon became apparent that I was the cause of most of the mishaps. Unfortunately my brother, two years my senior, was frequently the casualty as a result of my complete disregard for 'health and safety' in the playground. After every incident the investigating officer – Mum – would mete out punishment to the perpetrator – myself. I feel that in ninety per cent of the cases my pain exceeded any that my brother had suffered by my hand. My mum could slap for England in those days and only stopped when she ran out of steam. The outhouse was my usual safe haven. If I could get there quickly enough I would scrabble beneath the copper.

The hearth, where logs were burned to heat the water, afforded just enough space for me to curl in a defensive ball. She would pace up and down – as a hound will when the fox has gone to ground – until her fiery mood subsided. She was a woman who quickly flew into a rage but just as quickly returned to normality; I suppose her manner could be termed as 'slap and cuddle', because she alternated between slapping and cuddling. As long as I could find refuge quickly enough I was OK. I believe she admired my spirit of survival.

There was never any grudge borne on either side. If I escaped punishment by being quick off the mark, the punishment was forgotten. Mum could never strike in cold blood. With this knowledge under my belt I was the quickest boy in the village when it came to performing a disappearing act. My brother, on the other hand, though slow to hide, was quick to reveal my hiding place, grassing me up to the investigating officer – Mum – who would then administer punishment. I eventually realised that punishment was applied with less fervour if my brother's tittle-tattling had instigated it. The relationship between my brother and me was no different from that of any other siblings. We would both try and win favour with Mum and Dad and if that meant getting each other into trouble, then so be it. There was no malice aforethought employed in the pranks we played on each other but very often it took all of the fluttering eyelashes, innocent expressions and guile to convince either Mum or Dad that it was not me who was guilty. Unfortunately they were both aware that there was always more likelihood that I would be the root cause of every upset. I believe I gained a reputation for mischief at a very early age. We were two very different personalities and therefore tended to seek other playmates. This was probably the salvation of my brother when you consider my record for accidents.

Accident or Intent?

There was a swimming 'hole' in the section of the river Avon that flowed through our part of the village known as the Hatches. The villagers would gather there when the weather was favourable. The river at this point evolved into an area of shallow water, graduating to deeper water, before passing through the Hatches. The Hatches, so named because of the feature's function when it was part of an irrigation system, created an aqua-park that was ideal for adults and children. Adults only used this facility on high days and holidays, as their workload did not allow a great deal of time for leisure. We, the children, however, were always drawn to this aqua-park. One fine summer day we were all splashing and jumping in the river when someone cried, 'Water rat!' The children reacted quite dramatically. Girls screamed and ran, while the boys all grabbed large stones and started a bombardment. Unfortunately my brother was still in the river and directly in the line of fire.

His back was to me and he seemed frozen. My chosen missile was quite heavy but I managed to lob it in the general direction of the rat's last reported position. It seemed as though everything reverted to slow motion. The rock soared slowly upwards through the air and, as it lost its trajectory, struck the back of my brother's head; he went face down into the water. My first thought was that he couldn't possibly know who had thrown the rock as his back was towards me at the time. The slow motion effect quickly changed to ultra speed. He leaped from the water and took off across the field in the general direction of the village. I knew I had to catch him before he could report to Mum. Scalp wounds bleed quite profusely and this wound was no exception. I was pounding along behind him and the blood was cascading down his bare back.

He was bellowing like a wounded animal and moving with the speed of a greyhound. I could not catch him. He was eventually stopped by two well-meaning adults and whisked off to their cottage for treatment.

The adults announced that they had witnessed one child, bleeding from a head wound and very distressed, being pursued by another child who was unmarked and who guiltily veered away when the adults rescued the injured child. Because all children were known in the village I was immediately identified. Once more I was brought before the investigating officer – Mum – and that was how the accidental stoning of my brother ended. Young Jim was accused, and convicted, of causing injury to his brother. The guilty party accepted his punishment stoically.

Another instance of brother abuse occurred when, on one occasion, he joined my best friend Mo – the neighbour's daughter – and me while we were holding races in the garden. The object was to start from the well and dash to the cherry tree. At the cherry tree, change one shoe for the other, and with your shoes now on the wrong feet race back to the well. My brother wanted to take part so we allowed him to join us. He was two years older than both of us and naturally won almost every race, all but the last one. I was annoyed by the fact that he continually beat us so on the last few yards of the race I gave him a great push. The windlass stanchions of the well were six-by-six-inch solid oak; the edges were not chamfered. It was one of these edges that my brother's forehead struck, thereby ending his headlong flight. The bellowing started immediately. This in itself was quite alarming, but it was the swelling that fascinated Mo and me. Our mothers were quickly on the scene, alerted by the bellowing, but they also became mesmerised by the rapid swelling. It was gathering momentum as we all looked on in amazement.

The lump was purple and red with a deep vertical groove. It grew relentlessly until the application of many cold compresses finally brought the grotesque swelling under control. Because of my fascination with the injury I had failed to make a quick exit; consequently, another example of my pain exceeding that of my brother's quickly followed. Even while in extreme pain he still managed to get the message across to Mum that I was the root cause once more. My brother gloated over my punishment but he did not express any further desire to join in our games or adventures for a very long time.

Hazelnuts and Moorhens' Eggs

Not every accident suffered by my brother was my fault. He developed a form of tuberculosis when he was ten years old; it necessitated the removal of a gland in his throat. He was taken into a cottage hospital that was situated on the edge of Savernake forest. It lay on the outskirts of Marlborough, about eight miles from our home – not a great distance today, but in those days it was very difficult to visit him. Mum would set out very early on her journey, which involved taking the short cut along the railway track to catch a bus from Pewsey. I was left in the care of our neighbour for the duration of her visit. After what must have been a tiring and traumatic day she would return and tell us of his progress and how well he was being cared for.

A few days into his internment Mum came back from her daily visit almost in tears. He had been placed in a side ward – this was a room that was separated from the main ward by a glass partition. There was a door in the partition for access. Above my brother's bed and attached to the partition was a shelf on which an open two-bar electric fire was positioned. A nurse had been tending him and on leaving the ward had slammed the door a little too hard. The resulting vibration caused the fire to be dislodged and it fell on to my brother's chest.

Thankfully I was not on the premises at the time; for once I was blameless.

He still bears the scars from the burns, yet the scar on his neck from the operation is barely discernable. Mum was so grateful that her son was in hospital when the accident happened! Friends and neighbours all expressed the same platitudes: 'Thank goodness he was in hospital when it happened'; 'He couldn't have been in a better place'; 'At least he was in the right place'. It is obvious that the compensation culture had not gathered the momentum in the forties that it has in the present time. I am quite certain that my brother would argue that he could have been in a better place and that he most certainly was not in the right place at the time. Mum said that the matron, when relating the facts of the accident to her, seemed a little offhand, but that was quite understandable as the matron was a very busy woman!

During his internment I accompanied my mother on one of her visits to cheer him up but I quickly became bored. After verifying that he was in a reasonable condition I was allowed to go to the day room to amuse myself. I was happily chatting and playing with the other children when I noticed that the centre table was being laid for tea. When a nurse came into the room and proceeded to question me – 'What is your name?' 'How old are you?' 'Where are you from?' – I readily gave her the answers. Once she had taken the information from me she told me to take a seat at the table. This was an adult in uniform, an authority figure; I quite naturally did as I was told. I was soon presented with afternoon tea. I remember it vividly because of the sandwich; it was thin, filled with jam and cut into triangles.

My mother was not renowned for presentation when it came to making sandwiches. Dad always referred to them as 'doorsteps', very nutritious and satisfying, but lacking in elegance. I was impressed with the hospital version and quickly devoured the lot.

Once satisfied I left the day room and returned to Mum, who was about to say her goodbyes before leaving. The next day she went to the hospital alone, one visit being enough for me, where she was told in no uncertain terms that I had been the cause of pandemonium the evening before. The nurse, who had taken my particulars assuming that I was a new patient, was dutifully processing me for admission to the children's ward. When she returned to collect me I had disappeared. The immediate reaction was to raise the alarm; they had not just lost a patient but a child patient to boot. The hospital authorities were not pleased and, unfortunately, Mum bore the brunt. I was not repentant, as the sandwich had been given to me freely. A hungry boy was hardly likely to refuse, especially when it was the prettiest sandwich I had ever seen.

Mum continued to visit my brother as many times as she could while he was in the hospital but it was decided that my visit was a one-off and never to be repeated. I was not too perturbed by this decision. There were so many adventures to be experienced with my friends, visiting a sick brother was a long way down my list of priorities. We had fields to explore and minnows to be caught; sticklebacks were lurking in the streams just waiting to be trapped in a jam jar and transported home for further examination; hospital visiting was nothing when compared with that. Although I carried

Hazelnuts and Moorhens' Eggs

on as though he was not around my heart was not in the usual day-to-day activities until he came home.

I was very attentive towards my brother when he was finally discharged from the hospital. There was little doubt that he was quite poorly after the operation and this, coupled with the quite severe burns to his chest, led me to feel that he was entitled to a bit of sibling respect and support. I don't remember how long my sympathetic attitude lasted but I dare say it wasn't long before we were back to our usual tormenting and tittle-tattling.

Safe Havens

Secret hiding places were paramount in my childhood. One such haven, equally as secure as the copper hearth, was the box hedge that formed the boundary between our garden and the road. The hedge was very dense and ran the full length of the garden. Concealed in its immaculately trimmed sides were many secret entrances. I had to protect my eyes on entering as dust and cobwebs were an integral part of its make-up. Once inside I would wriggle my way deeply into its welcoming darkness. I recall one frightening incident where the hedge played a very important part in my sense of security.

Due to the events of the war, propaganda was part of everyday life and we were always made aware that the Germans could invade at any time. As children, we were not sure what Germans would look like or what vehicles or guises they would employ. Would they eat children? Would they shoot everybody on sight? Perhaps they would burn everything in their path? I'm sure you will agree that these were nerve-racking times for any five-year-old. Adults did their best to prevent us from overhearing their apprehensive conversations, but as the saying goes, 'Little pitchers have big ears.'

The war had been over for a few months when, as if to emphasise the beginning of a new era, a very decorative ice-cream van paid a visit to our village. My first impression was of a brightly coloured gold-and-silver weapon of war careering down our narrow country road. This was accompanied by the ringing of what I believed to be alarm bells. I had never seen or tasted ice cream and was not about to stay around to be slaughtered by the German army. I took to the box hedge, burrowing much deeper than I ever had before, then climbing upward in my efforts to avoid detection.

The noise increased as the van drew closer to our cottage until the vehicle finally stopped opposite my hiding place. I was

Hazelnuts and Moorhens' Eggs

trembling with fear but decided to push my head up through the top of the hedge to have a quick peep. I remember that it was the colour of the vehicle that first caught my attention; I had never expected an armoured car or tank to be so brightly painted. The van was glittering with gold and silver. The bodywork was coloured deep maroon and adorned with headlights of silver; these were polished to a dazzling finish. The canopy was made of a glossy white material supported by twisted columns of silver, in the style of sticks of barley sugar. Between the tops of the columns was emblazoned the logo, 'Rusher's Ice Cream'. It did not seem to present any threat but I was taking no chances. I could see the driver from my vantage point. He appeared to be quite normal and harmless. However, it was the lady in the back of the van that filled me with dread. She was very stocky with hair that was blacker than my mother's black lead range; it was drawn from her forehead to the nape of her neck in a severe style that I later discovered was Italian. Her lips were coated with extremely red lipstick and her eyes were like two black marbles. This woman had to be German. The dark aura that surrounded her was emphasised by a startling whiter-than-white overall. She was absolutely terrifying and I quickly and quietly withdrew into the sanctuary of my box hedge. It took many visits of the ice-cream van before I was convinced that this was a friend and not a foe.

Another example of the box hedge providing sanctuary for me occurred in what came to be known as the 'match ball incident'. My dad was team manager, and player, for the village football team. Among his duties – pitch marking, organising venues etc., was the responsibility for the match ball (it was the only ball they had).

After every match he diligently pumped the ball up, laced it, applied dubbin and stored it in a cupboard in our cottage until the next match day. One day my friend Mo and I decided to take the ball and have a game of football in the road. We were having a great time, oblivious to the scuffmarks that were appearing on the leather. Unfortunately a bus that came through the village only once a week appeared at the top of the road. We had chosen the only day that it was due. It trundled towards us and as we took to the bank for safety it ran over the match ball. The ball burst with a resounding bang. The bus carried on, the driver unaware, or maybe not, of the damage he had done. As the bus disappeared from view I was left with the belief that the driver was a member of an opposing village football team! We stood in stunned silence. My Uncle Todd had recently given me a genuine leather pilot helmet with matching goggles. These items had proved indispensable for protecting my eyes and ears in the box hedge in practice. Now the time had come to put them to the test in a real incident.

We waited long enough to confirm that there would be no football match for some time and then ran for cover. I quickly donned the helmet and goggles and took to the hedge while Mo played the feminine card and skipped home to her mother. I stayed in the box hedge for an eternity that time; I believe I fell asleep. I hadn't only upset my dad but also all the other members and fans of the football team. They were soon demanding that Dad should punish me by giving me a really good hiding. I think it was their demands that made my dad take my side. Boys will be boys and nobody was going to tell my dad what to do, especially when it concerned his family. I believe he viewed the incident as proof of my desire to become a professional footballer. Needless to say the match ball was never to be taken from its cupboard again, unless it was by Dad.

Another safe haven for me was the family toilet. Situated at the top of the garden the 'dunnock', as it was known, often provided me with a hiding place. It was built of well-seasoned planks of wood with a few small knotholes dotted around its sides. These holes, as well as providing much-needed ventilation, were also a means of keeping a sharp lookout. The dunnock was a work of art. The seating arrangement was designed for adults and children, a 'two holer', side by side, one large and one small. The woodwork was scrubbed to a snow-white finish and the door latch was positioned low to enable a child to gain access without the need of assistance from an adult. It was the last place that Mum would look as it was considered a pretty unsavoury place to spend any time, other than to obey the call of nature. I liked it, but it could not match the womb-like security of the box hedge, as the chance of a surprise visit by Mum always existed.

Hazelnuts and Moorhens' Eggs

My best friend and companion was Mo, the daughter of our next-door neighbour. We were the same age and today would be referred to as being joined at the hip. Her mother was known to me as 'Mudder' and was my second mum in every way. I had a great fondness for her. Her tolerance of some of the escapades that Young Jim and Mo became involved in was amazing. I realise that we all have greater tolerance for other people's children than our own, but Mudder was exceptional.

In our little world, Mo was always known as Joe and I was Bill. One day Bill and Joe found a box of matches – perhaps purloined would be a more appropriate word. The matches were out of bounds to children. We knew we were not allowed to play with them but the spirit of adventure won the day. At the rear of the cottage was the woodpile, a stock of logs and kindling, fuel for the range and copper. It was here that we decided to experiment with the matches: recipe for disaster.

For the mixture: take a hot summer day – add dry kindling – some dry grass – two children – a box of matches – and a thatched cottage. Who needed Germans?

This was the only time that my refuge was ill chosen. As the thatch inevitably ignited I knew that we had really gone too far this time and I could almost feel the stinging contact of my mum's hand. My survival instinct kicked in and I headed for a hiding place. With the misplaced wisdom of a five-year-old, I dashed into the cottage, up the stairs and sought refuge under my mum's bed. As had proved prudent in similar circumstances, I had been very quick off the mark and no one had seen my break for safety. There was a building beyond our garden, a corrugated shed that operated as a commercial garage. The location afforded the proprietor a good view of our cottage and, as he was the only car owner in the village, he was very rarely busy. Luckily, alerted by screams and a plume of smoke, he witnessed the fire take hold.

He reacted swiftly and rushed to the rescue with his stirrup pump. With my mum and Mudder acting as water carriers, the water having to be drawn from the well, the fire was eventually brought under control. Punishment for that incident was suspended due to my mother's relief on finding me safe and sound, albeit scared witless. My fear was of my mum's wrath and not of perishing in what could have been a blazing inferno. Someone up there was looking after me. Mo was also forgiven for her part in our one and only experiment with combustible materials and the matches were given a new hiding place.

The only other unfortunate happening in the kindling and wood store involved the use of a billhook. Bill and Joe were once more the main players. We had decided to help our mothers by chopping firewood, or preparing kindling for the range. This was normally a chore undertaken only by adults but we decided it was not beyond our capabilities.

The billhook Dad used was not of the common type. The basic shape was the same but this one had an additional four-inch-by-two-inch raised section on the reverse edge of the hook. This was sharpened giving the billhook the advantage of having a dual purpose: it served as a billhook on one side and, when used on the reverse, it served as an axe. It was quite a heavy tool even for an adult; in my little hands it was extremely heavy. Bill and Joe were steadily chopping firewood and looking forward to the praise that would be heaped upon them for their ability and kindness in helping their parents. Perhaps my little arms were becoming weary, or I had grown a little too confident. On my raising the billhook above my head for a final swing downwards the hook dropped from my hands and struck me on the top of the head. If the billhook had been of the usual design no harm would have been done, but the axe section of Dad's billhook connected with the top of my head and caused quite a substantial cut. As on many other occasions, I had suffered a minor injury while embarking on a well-intentioned deed, the main reason for which was to win the admiration and praise of my parents. It always seemed to backfire and instead of praise I was frequently rewarded with punishment. I realise that much of the punishment was meted out as a knee-jerk reaction, triggered by relief that I hadn't come to more harm than I had.

Not every adventure or game that Bill and Joe became involved in was fraught with danger. We had many hilarious outings. We were once with our mothers on a visit to the nearby town of Pewsey to collect essential groceries. It was quite common to see troop movements through the town in convoys of

Hazelnuts and Moorhens' Eggs

army trucks. These brave lads were always regaled with friendly good wishes and waves and on this particular day they responded by releasing balloons from the rear of their trucks.

Not being familiar with balloons we quickly took advantage of the generosity of these friendly soldiers. Gathering as many of the balloons as we could we did not consider it unusual that they were all the same pale off-white colour, or that the mouthpiece was rather large; as stated, we had never seen a balloon before, we were just happy to have the opportunity to collect these unique objects to play with. I can only assume that our mothers found it less embarrassing to go along with the soldiers' prank than explain to two five-year-olds what a condom was really used for. They allowed us to keep them after the convoy had gone, and even take them home with us. It was probably part of their wartime 'make do and mend' philosophy. After all, a balloon is only an inflated rubber sleeve whichever way you look at it and owing to the density of the material our pseudo-balloons were not destined to last for very long.

It was common for Bill and Joe to play in the confines of the gardens of our adjoined cottages. The gardens were very large by today's standards, as they had to provide enough produce to feed a family throughout the year. Not only did the garden sustain the family but it also served as a storage area. Firewood, tools, chicken hutches and castaway boxes and bins all helped to create secret places for two young reprobates to amuse themselves. The further away from the watchful eyes of their mothers the better. Completely out of sight of mothers is a myth though – the all-seeing eye of a mother is omnipotent, as Bill and Joe so often learnt.

We discovered our biological differences very early in our young lives, a natural thing for two healthy youngsters playing together for the majority of every day. It was noted at a very early age that Joe always had a wee in a crouched position, while Bill could manage the same performance standing upright. A competition was soon devised to see who could wee the furthest in either position.

I can honestly say that Joe always bested Bill in both categories. Our interest in each other's bits and pieces widened, and our playtime activities became more and more adult in content. It was not long before the omniscient eye of Mum witnessed it all and signalled a halt to any further escapades. A little parental guidance was applied and Bill and Joe wisely reverted to the earlier games that had been the foundation of their playtime partnership, more mischievous in content perhaps, but more in keeping with the behaviour expected of five-year-olds.

In the bird-nesting season we indulged in a more mischievous game of mix and match. There was little need for a cuckoo while Bill and Joe were on the loose. The object of this game was to locate as many nests in the area as we could. Hedgerows, all of which contained an abundance of birds' nests, provided easy pickings for such as Bill and Joe. Hedgerows concealing nests bordered every lane, field and garden. Many of these hedges were comprised of hawthorn and very often during the nesting season boys were asked to raise their sleeves by their schoolteachers for an inspection of their forearms; the scratches on their arms immediately revealed evidence of bird-nesting activities.

Although it was not an offence to gather eggs, it was severely frowned on by many lovers of wildlife, and schoolteachers tried to shame boys into giving up the practice by berating them before the rest of the class. I was very often both shamed and berated!

Bill and Joe would take an egg from one nest and exchange it for another; the only criterion was that the eggs differed in either colour or size. The variety of bird that had laid the egg did not concern us. Blackbirds hatching hedge sparrows and thrushes hatching robins, this was integration in its true form. In most cases our interest dwindled before any results were noted.

We never really discovered if our species of the genus 'cuckoo' was successful as there was always more mischief to be getting into. Watching eggs hatch would probably equate to watching paint dry today. I hadn't aspired to forming an egg collection in those early years. That activity would come later as a genuine interest in bird life and other aspects of nature gathered momentum. Besides, there were far more interesting and exciting activities for us to engage in. Discovering gender differences through intensive body exploration in the dark confines of the dunnock for example. Bill and Joe were more than just good mates.

Hazelnuts and Moorhens' Eggs

The soot bag was another magnet to Bill and Joe. Whenever the chimney was swept the soot was put aside to spread on the garden, a very beneficial additive to the soil according to gardeners. For us, it was a very detrimental additive to our child/parent relationship. It seemed that whenever the soot magnet tempted us, it coincided with washday. Washday was the day when Mum's zero tolerance came into force. Everything went on hold on washing day; the whole day was devoted solely to laundering. The copper had to be filled from the well. The log fire had to be prepared under the copper to heat the water and the beds stripped of sheets. The sheets were always placed first into the copper, as they needed the longest drying time on the washing line and so, when the water was hot enough a block of soap was added, followed by the sheets. With powerful prods of the copper-stick and the addition of a 'blue bag' to enhance whiteness the weekly process would get underway. When the sheets were boiled to Mum's satisfaction she would remove, rinse, and pass them through the wringer, or mangle as it was known, and from there to the washing line in the garden. Depending on the wind speed and direction, this could be comparatively easy, or very difficult.

Once they were secured with clothes pegs, purchased from the gypsies who hawked them door to door, the copper was topped up with water and the next batch would begin. The drying sheets would crack and snap noisily like man-o'-war sails in a brisk wind, an audible and visual experience you will not get from a modern day tumble dryer! For Mum to have to endure this hard labour was bad enough, but when confronted by Bill and Joe, plus a bag of soot, you can understand how she rapidly reached breaking point.

We were too young to understand wind direction and the effect it would have on fine grains of soot, or of the effect of wind and soot in unison coming into contact with damp sheets. We were too happily engaged tossing the soot into the air to be aware of Mum's breaking point being rapidly approached. We very quickly became aware however, when Mum appeared, roaring up the garden path, in pursuit of the two Al Jolson lookalikes! The copper was in use that day so there was no hiding under its protective wing. Joe made it to safety but this was one occasion when Bill bore the brunt of the frustrations of washing day. To say it was a lesson learnt would be untrue as the same thing occurred a few weeks later. Bill and Joe's denial of any participation in playing with soot intensified the punishment. The resemblance to black-and-white minstrels while trying to appear innocent did nothing to help their case. The handprints on my legs for that incident resembled Braille. Whenever Bill and Joe as a team committed a misdemeanour, it seemed that only Bill received punishment. Mudder, Mo's mum, was never on the scene when we were caught. It was always my mum and she would not lay a finger on another person's child. It would be years before I learnt that it was better to own up immediately than to prolong the suspense.

Mum was a very difficult woman to lie to. She would stare directly into my eyes while keeping a tenacious grip on my arms. Once she was satisfied that I was completely mesmerised by her startling blue eyes she would demand to be told the truth. On one occasion I was given my pyjamas and a penny and told to sit on the doorstep until the dustman came to take me away. I assume the fee to remove little boys who told lies was a penny.

Parenting was different in those days. There was no way that I could threaten to report my mum to any well-meaning authority, or for her to have any fear that a well-meaning neighbour would call some controlling body to rescue me from the situation. Surprise surprise, despite the apparent lack of Mum's parenting skills, when compared to the assessments of latter-day 'professionals', it seems she has managed to raise four children who are happier, more well adjusted and respectful of all aspects of authority. She was not in the minority; most parents of that era raised their families in the same manner. Extra guidance could be obtained from grandparents, as nature intended. The majority of families were indigenous to the area and the extended family was always close by to offer advice and guidance, sometimes not always welcome. They were, nevertheless, a reliable source of knowledge, there to be drawn upon when other means began to falter.

My grandparents on both sides of the family passed away

before I was born, so I never had the benefit of being treated as a grandchild. The emotion that I experienced when watching those of my friends with their grandparents was envy. Grandparents always had patience; they also seemed to have a never-ending supply of sweets. They all looked cuddly and they emitted a wonderful homely smell, new bread and vapour rub being among the most memorable ingredients to me. They all wore the most amazing slippers and the grannies all wore wrap-around aprons. There is no doubt that I did miss having a grandfather or grandmother during my childhood.

Return of the Gladiators

The menfolk started to arrive back in the village a few at a time, their service to king and country completed. I was a babe in arms when my dad was conscripted, so my recountable knowledge of him began with his demobilisation. He was a loving and affectionate character and gave my brother and me a feeling of great security, and at long last we were a proper family.

As a country boy himself he deemed it his duty to educate us in the ways of the countryside. This involved teaching us, among other things, how to procure food from the fields and hedgerows. At this he was a master. His way of imparting this knowledge was to include us in his foraging. It was poaching in reality, but to him it was a countryman's basic right. There were no serious confrontations with the local farmers and it was acceptable to roam their hedgerows and fields. Rabbits were the main fare of the majority of country folk. Those that couldn't catch them themselves would gladly pay Dad a few pence for one. This was quite a lucrative little earner for him and he would actually hunt to order for the more expensive pheasant or partridge. Rabbits were blatantly hung around his waist when caught but pheasant, partridge and duck were always secreted in various pouches about his person. Even though there was little or no confrontation with the landowner, it was wiser to keep some things under wraps. The rabbit was a pest, and plentiful, but the fact that the expression 'breed like a pheasant' has never existed will give some indication why it was better not to advertise their procurement.

Dad would never take both of his boys hunting at the same time. He had a saying that he applied to any situation where it was necessary to hold a young boy's attention: 'If you have one boy – you have a boy. If you have two boys – you have half a boy. If you have three boys – you have no boys at all.'

To aid Dad with his poaching activities he possessed many accessories. His armoury consisted of one twelve-gauge shotgun,

Hazelnuts and Moorhens' Eggs

one folding .410-gauge shotgun and one .22 rifle.

He always carried a catapult himself and taught me how to make a very efficient catapult of my own. This I dutifully carried for the majority of my childhood, as did most boys of the period. There were rabbit snares, or wires as he called them, together with gin traps, purse nets for covering boltholes when ferreting, and ferrets housed in a hutch in the garden. There were long poles with snares attached for snaring roosting pheasants, paper cones for catching feeding pheasants and horsehair for threading through plump raisins to choke unwary pheasants. He also owned a custom-made cape with numerous hidden pockets for the concealment of the more sophisticated catch. After the fur and feather equipment came the fishing tackle; this was a collection of fishing rods, hand lines and night lines and included the fingers of both hands, used for tickling trout.

I recall one poaching occasion that reinforced my belief in the existence of a greater being, or one who keeps a protective eye on events here in the mortal world. My dad had opted to take me with him on this particular day; it was more common for me to accompany him than my brother. I believe that my enthusiasm for this type of pastime was greater than his. It was sure to be tutorial but I would also be expected to double as a retriever, provided the quarry didn't fall into brambles or nettles. In the 1940s a boy did not have the luxury of long trousers, as was evident from the scabs, scratches and nettle rash that adorned most active boys' legs. Dad never expected me to retrieve from rough areas.

We had been wandering the hedgerows for a couple of hours, with a few rabbits to our credit, when we reached a stile. I crossed first and Dad passed the .22 rifle to me, an act of irresponsibility that today would have had me taken from him and placed in care.

Dad was burdened with rabbits so it was safer for him to use both hands to cross the stile and then collect the rifle from me. A .22 rifle is a fairly lightweight weapon in the hands of an adult, but to a boy of tender years it proved a little cumbersome. As my dad was crossing the stile, the rifle slipped through my grip. The weight of the rifle drove the muzzle into the soft earth of the field. I jerked it free and was greatly relieved to notice that Dad hadn't seen what had happened, his back being towards me at the time.

A boy of my age could not have known the effect of firing a rifle if the barrel is blocked. In fact there are many adults who would be unaware of the consequences. I was torn between saying nothing, and hopefully not incurring his wrath, or owning up and facing the consequences. In any other circumstance I know I would have said nothing. My philosophy had always been to deny anything that might bring punishment and it had always worked. This time however there was a nagging feeling that I should mention to him that I had accidentally poked the barrel into the ground. I grasped the nettle and in a matter-of-fact little voice told him what had happened. He upended the rifle and sure enough, the barrel was well and truly plugged with dirt. I cringed, expecting all manner of wrath to descend upon my head; instead he quietly selected a fine twig from the hedgerow and cleared the barrel. When he did react it was to heap praise and gratitude on me for having had the courage to warn him. I did not know the barrel was blocked, or what could have happened had he fired it, but something or someone gave me the right guidance that day.

There have been a few times in life when I knew that some guardian angel or greater being was definitely watching over me. It has been both rewarding and reassuring to have concrete added to the foundations of a belief.

After a successful outing gathering food for the table we would make our way home. This was the next step in the education of the young hunter-gatherer. The preparation of the 'bag' was always fascinating for me. It's strange that later in life I would choose the navy as a career and not express a desire to become a surgeon! Dad would pluck and draw the pheasants and skin and paunch the rabbits. Pigeons were divested of their breast feathers only. Then the breast fillets would be removed and the carcasses committed to the runner bean trench; nothing was wasted. Jointing the rabbits without creating bone splinters was an art. While Dad was completing these tasks he would show me the skeletal structure and internal organs, explaining the functions of each and which were the best to eat. If you haven't eaten rabbit kidneys you haven't lived.

Hazelnuts and Moorhens' Eggs

I was emulating my dad when I presented Mum with the blackbird. Although she was horrified by my action I did overhear her relating the story to our neighbour and grudgingly admitting that, despite being barbaric, I had done quite a professional job.

To this day I have the urge to bone every joint of meat that my wife brings home from the butcher. I always completely bone our Christmas turkey, stuff it with a boned chicken and sew it up to resemble its original form before cooking. I realise that it is all due to the teachings of my dad over sixty years ago in the little scullery of our cottage.

It was an idyllic lifestyle for a growing boy and the lessons learnt from that time have stood me in good stead on many occasions. I am confident that if circumstances demanded that I live off the land to survive I would do so very successfully. My dad was not an academic; however, he taught me everything that he deemed important, drawn from the experiences of his own passage through life. He would never be able to help me with my school homework but the term 'horses for courses' was made for him.

Of all the poaching activities, ferreting was my favourite. Preparing for the venture always brought about an air of excitement as Dad collected everything that would be needed for the day: purse nets, extra pegs and a mallet, halters and long lines, spade, shotgun and plenty of warm clothes. The best ferrets for the day were selected, placed in the ferret sack, and we were ready. Our Uncle Todd usually accompanied us on such days as these. He was as much a poacher as Dad but more experimental in his technique. It was Uncle Todd who first tried the corn-filled paper cone to catch pheasants.

His idea was to make a cone from a sheet of paper – A4 size would be appropriate. He would place corn in the base then smear grease or any other sticky substance around the wider end. The prepared cone would then be stood in the grass in an area where pheasants were known to forage. The theory was that the pheasant, on finding the cone, would reach in to gather the corn and the grease would stick the cone to its feathers. When it tried to retract its head the cone would become a hood and, like a falcon, it would sit quietly until Uncle Todd arrived and gently picked it up.

He also made some very strange concoctions. Had we been in America I suppose you might say it was moonshine; however, a waste product of this sideline came in the form of fat, alcohol-soaked raisins. He would laboriously thread a horsehair through each raisin and scatter them where pheasants were known to forage. The theory here was that the pheasants (those not already wearing paper dunce hats) would swallow the raisin, choke on the horsehair and once again Uncle Todd would be on hand to collect them. He served in the Royal Air Force for the duration of the war, and I think their quest for new innovations left a lasting impression on Uncle Todd. He never tried to bring a new approach to ferreting though, much to my dad's relief. I suppose the ferret could not be improved upon, despite the inventiveness of the RAF.

After a final check we would gather up the required equipment between us and set off across the fields to a warren that Dad had selected for the day. On our arrival, a search of the surrounding area would be carried out. Every likely place that could conceal a bolthole was examined and, hopefully, every bolthole would be covered with a purse net. A stake driven into the ground secured the net. There were many times, even after diligently locating and securing what we considered to be every bolthole, when we would be surprised by a rabbit leaping from a bed of nettles and making a break for freedom. Dad usually curtailed the break with a well-aimed shot from the twelve-bore.

Once Dad was happy with the preparations the ferret would be introduced into the burrow. He always preferred letting the ferret go in without a tether. This was sometimes frustrating when the ferret decided to stay below ground or exit from the bolthole that we had all missed but with the lead or tether, there was the danger of the ferret passing through tree roots or other underground obstructions, backtracking, then proceeding forward again and creating an intricate knot that could not be untangled. The spade would have to be used to recover the ferret and the day would end with nothing to show for the efforts of Dad and his helpers.

Once the ferret was in the burrow we would all squat and wait. This to me was the best part. In complete silence we would wait with ears tuned for the expected rumbling that a rabbit makes when it is chased from its habitat. I can still feel the excitement and tension that built up. When the rabbits finally bolted I would be startled as they burst from the ground and become entangled in the purse nets. We learnt to suffer the ribald comments directed at us from Dad when a rabbit escaped from an undetected bolthole. No matter how many times I was taken ferreting the excitement for me was always the same.

When we had gathered all of the rabbits and they had been dispatched with a quick jerk of the neck, a procedure that I was too small to perform, Dad would paunch them. They would be 'hocked': this was a procedure that involved cutting a slit between the lower leg bone and the tendon. The other leg would be pushed through the aperture and the rabbit could be carried on a stick or belt with ease.

After collecting the equipment it would be time to head for home. Mum would have something ready for us to eat once the skinning and jointing of the day's catch was done. What a great way to enjoy the countryside! These were the halcyon days before myxomatosis had severely depleted the rabbit population. Myxomatosis, I believe introduced from Australia deliberately by man, was a disease that deprived the average country family of a convenient and nutritious source of food.

Not every foraging activity performed by Dad was for food. Money, or the lack of it, was always a worry and I remember one attempt by Dad at earning extra cash that involved entering the fur trade on a very minor scale. I have to say that none of these schemes seemed strange to me or my brother, it was a way of life; the head of the family did everything in his power to nurture and supply the household. The furrier career did not last too long as I believe the ends did not justify the means. Dad was the middleman whose role it was to supply pelts. The pelts were taken from moles, moleskin coats being quite fashionable at the time. He would set off across the fields with a garden hoe and a sack. A huge scarf would be wound around his neck to protect him during the chilly wait. The moles were detected by finding a field where molehills were in evidence. Once this was achieved it was a matter of patiently watching and waiting until the movement of earth indicated the presence of a mole. The hoe was used to strike quickly to unearth the mole while taking great care to avoid damaging the animal's fur.

Speed was of prime importance to prevent the mole going to earth. I was never included in the mole-catching outings. I believe that Dad applied the rule that, as it was not a food gathering operation, there was no reason for him to teach me. I would have to make extra cash using my own methods when I had a family of my own to support.

After a very long absence Dad would return with the catch, never a great number as I recall, and warm himself before the black lead range with a mug of tea. The next step was skinning the moles. Surprisingly I was never invited to witness this. I was actively encouraged to skin and prepare every other type of animal that was destined for the table, but the preparation of the mole was a no-go area as far as Dad was concerned. Perhaps my parents thought that the little furry creature resembled a storybook character, and therefore would not be a suitable sight for a child to witness. The skins were pinned on to a board and placed in a sunny position to dry. There must have been many other procedures before the skins could be sold, but the whole process held little interest for me. I do remember a figure of a shilling for six skins being quoted, but it was a venture that did not last very long. Dabbling in the fur trade was not lucrative enough for Dad so it was a return to poaching to order.

I have very little recollection of rain during my childhood. Obviously there was rain, but my life was either too idyllic to be spoiled by the memory of it, or it was insignificant in the grand order of my childhood adventures. However, I do remember thunderstorms and the fear of being struck by lightning. We would dash wildly across fields with tiny hands trying to cover anything metallic about our person; it was usually the 'snake belt buckle'. We had been told of the need to avoid taking shelter under trees but were also aware of lightning's attraction to metal.

Even the deluge that must have accompanied these electrical storms has not registered in my memory. I can remember wet feet however; hardly a day went by without getting wet feet. It was inevitable when you realise that a large part of our adventure park

Hazelnuts and Moorhens' Eggs

consisted of rivers, water meadows, ditches, streams and even cattle troughs. Whenever I returned home after playing in water, I would foolishly try to avoid Mum's attention. Attempts to dry my socks by beating them on the river bridge wall always failed. A wet woollen sock will stretch to about twice its normal length when it is swung against a hard surface, an obvious clue for a watchful mother, but the swinging does not even dry the sock completely, so if Mum missed the concertina effect of the stretched socks she would certainly detect the steam arising from them. Sitting too close to the range was a mistake that I frequently made. When the first spectral wisps of steam from my wet socks started to rise, Mum, like some ghost whisperer or medium, would spot it and once again the punishment would be meted out. Mum was never fooled.

I never learnt my lesson; my childhood continued to be a combination of wet feet, scabbed knees and, on one occasion, what was to be diagnosed as sunstroke. The streams and ditches were filled with minnows, sticklebacks, frogs and watercress and with the aid of jam jars and nets we would catch these in abundance. If we grew thirsty during our activities we would search for a spot where a spring could be seen bubbling up through the streambed. We would immerse our faces in the spring water and drink our fill. Everything was clean and pure with no harmful pollution to worry about. We would gather watercress and dandelion leaves to take home and, depending on the time of year, collect pigeons' eggs for Mum. Dandelion and watercress salad with hard-boiled pigeons' eggs: what could be better? I remember these adventures but I cannot picture myself, I have to use my imagination.

It has to be imagination for the truth is that I have little or no idea of how I looked as a child. I know that I must have had fair hair and was perhaps 'well covered' to use my mother's terminology, but that is where it ends. Photographs were not commonplace then, and to own a camera was way beyond the means of many families. The only photograph that I have of myself is one taken for my father to take to war with him. It portrays me sat on Mum's knee with my brother stood alongside. There was nothing reflective in the cottage to allow me to obtain an image of myself; no pictures or mirrors were placed at child's height. The only mirror, or 'looking glass', was in Mum's room. Even a few years later, with the advent of the school photograph it was not my mother's way to preserve pictorial records. Once the heat from the fireplace had caused the photo to curl up, which in its position on the mantel shelf was inevitable, it was discarded. This was the destiny of all early photographs of my family, as Mum had no regard for posterity.

I imagine I was a mucky urchin most of the time because I was frequently treated to the 'spit and lick' wash that all mothers seemed adept at performing on their offspring at every given opportunity. Of all the ministrations my mother subjected me to, the spit and lick was the worst. It was almost an addiction in Mum's case. If a visitor appeared on the path to the cottage I was grabbed and held while Mum quickly spat on to her handkerchief and almost took the skin off of my face in her attempts to make me presentable. It could happen without warning at any time with Mum. It was, and probably to this day still is, the most annoying act that a mother can commit. I have witnessed the same pattern of behaviour among the mothers of today, so it was not peculiar to the mothers of the forties and fifties. Whenever I see the 'spit and lick' applied I know what the child is feeling. I have been there so many times.

Extending the Boundaries

There were some restrictions on our play areas because of our ages. I had not yet reached the age where I was allowed access to the Kennet and Avon canal or 'the Cut' as it was known locally. This was big boys' domain and a rite of passage for the seven-years-and-above age group.

The canal wended its way through the Wiltshire countryside, its course taking it about two miles north of our village. The distance of two miles was a measurement that denoted the age group that were allowed to play there.

It was the 'Academy of First-Time Achievements for Boys' and provided a boy with a host of new and educational experiences. It marked the beginning of a new chapter in the life of every country boy. Many new adventures started here, both in and on the still waters of the Cut. It was a chapter of many different but educational paragraphs.

My dad first taught me how to fish in the tackle-snagging, weedy waters of the canal.

I first learnt how to swim between the lock gates in the murky waters of the canal.

I had to eat the first tench that I caught in the canal – not a very palatable fish!

I gathered my first moorhen's eggs from the reed-covered nests in the canal – far more palatable than the tench.

I built and paddled my first raft on the canal.

My first fishing pole was a hazelnut branch taken from the coppices that bordered a large number of the towpaths of the canal. The hazelwood coppices for us were valuable assets. The wood furnished us with everything from fishing rods to bows and arrows and from pirates' swords to vaulting poles. The catalogue of uses was unending: 'If there's something you must fix, go and fetch some hazel sticks.'

Dad cut the pole for me and with a length of carpet thread, a quill float and a hook I was taken and taught the rudiments of fishing. These are the things that cement bonds between father and son. I couldn't say if it was the fishing tuition, or the fact that Dad was sharing his time with me that made it so enjoyable. I know that fishing could have been learnt by other means, and eventually, with or without his teaching, I would no doubt have become a perfectly proficient fisherman. I know with great certainty that the feelings that I hold for my dad could only have stemmed from his teaching, caring and bonding. He was with me the day I caught my first tench. The tench is a majestic fish and was regarded as the fish to get a boy elevated from fisher-boy to fisherman. Bream, perch, roach or rudd were merely fish. The tench, however, was the king, held in even higher esteem than the pike.

I was fishing close to the bridge on our stretch of the canal and Dad was about to leave me to go to his work. He had come with me to get me started in the early hours of the morning. As he was about to leave he spotted a tench blow near weeds on the far side. A tench blow is very easily identified by its dense mass of bubbles. It bears a remarkable similarity to a mass of floating frog spawn. He instructed me to 'Dap on it'. I did as he said and within seconds the float was away. The next command from Dad was, 'Hit it.'

I struck with all the enthusiasm of a whip-cracking muleskinner. The tench flew over my head and landed halfway up the bank, much to Dad's disgust. The fish measured just within the legal length at which it could be taken from the water. Dad pocketed it and took it home and on my return Mum had it ready to cook for my breakfast. It would have been kinder to me, and the fish, to leave it in the canal. Some people enjoy eating tench but the flavour resembles the habitat in which it lives: mud, clay and decaying organisms.

The canal towpath was like the pathway to adventure. The pillboxes that were placed at various intervals along its length were dark, damp, prison-like buildings. They were never used in anger during the war, but served a very useful purpose in peacetime. They served as the fisherman's emergency toilets, they became a convenient shelter in rainstorms during fishing competitions and a

Hazelnuts and Moorhens' Eggs

place of concealment for those courting couples that chose to wander along the towpath. The towpath was not wide enough to walk hand in hand so the privacy of the pillbox was a welcome haven.

In many places adjacent to the path were hazelwood coppices. It was here that we gathered the majority of our hazelnut harvest. The nuts would be dislodged from their husks by frenzied shaking of the branches. Young hunter-gatherers would descend on these coppices when the nuts were ready, and in the gloom that was ever present beneath the leafy bowers, perform the ritual shaking of the branches and gathering of the hazelnuts. The fruits of our labours were taken home, there to be enjoyed around the black lead range. It was around this range that Dad would tell us tales of his childhood and keep us amused with country quizzes of his own making. He would imitate, with incredible accuracy, animal and birdcalls for us to identify. Eventually, when we were tired and sated with hazelnuts, it would be time for Mum to light our way up the stairs to the bed that my brother and I shared. She always led the way with the oil lamp and tucked us in for the night. Once she was satisfied that we were settled she withdrew, and we were left in darkness until the next morning. I would snuggle under a host of blankets and relive that day's adventures while trying to decide on new adventures for the next day. There was always something to amuse a growing boy.

Although, in retrospect, my memories are viewed through rose-coloured glasses, there were a few unpleasant happenings. There was one instance while in the company of some of the older children of the village. A game of 'do chase' was taking place. The venue was a meadow located some distance from our usual play area, chosen because it was beyond the prying eyes of the adults. The object of the game was the same as 'kiss chase', but with a far greater adult connotation. A boy was designated to chase and catch one of the girls, and if successful, lie with her on the grass. The remainder would form a circle and, egging on the successful victor, watch while he proceeded to 'do' her. Eventually it was my turn to adopt the role as chaser. The conclusion was always the same; I always caught the same girl, mainly because she was the only one of my age and speed. When I had caught, performed, and completed my part, one of the older boys suddenly grabbed me by the arms and carried me to a nearby wasps' nest. He then waved me over the nest until the wasps began to gather in anger. The inevitable outcome for me was receiving approximately eight, or more, painful wasp stings on my bare legs. I ran home screaming with the pain and Mum applied first aid. First aid in this case was application of the blue bag to the stings. The blue bag, or blue cube, was designed to enhance the whiteness of the laundry and how it was supposed to calm wasp stings has always remained a mystery to me. However, it seemed to work. It probably had the same psychological effect as a placebo. The fact that I was not put off of sexual relations has also remained a mystery to me, but as far as I am aware, I have never made love near a wasps' nest since! After that ordeal the only time that I intentionally approached a wasps' nest was when Dad had poisoned the nest in his quest for the grubs. Wasp grubs make excellent fishing bait. After placing the poison in the entrance to the nest, we would stand clear. Once the poison had taken effect, Dad would dig up the nest and remove the grubs for future use.

Run Rabbit Run

A favourite period for me was harvest time. Every able-bodied man and boy in the village with the time to spare would gather in the wheat, corn or barley field that was ripe for harvesting. The binder would arrive. This was a horse-drawn reaping machine, which would be prepared for gathering in the harvest. We would assemble behind the binder with an assortment of clubs, some seasoned and well used, others just cut from the hedgerows. With a command from the operator the horse would start forward and the binder wheel would begin to turn as the machine gained momentum. It was similar in appearance to the propulsion unit of a paddle steamer but with a wheat field replacing the water. As the corn was pulled into the scissoring blade by the wheel it was cut, collected, and passed out of the side of the machine in sheaves. Farmhands following the binder gathered the sheaves and propped them in 'stooks', pyramid-shaped stacks of five, where they would remain until bundled up and taken to the thresher. The binder was a great labour-saving machine, the alternative, before its advent, being the scythe. Even so, harvesting still required a huge amount of manpower.

The attendance of the locals held its own reward, the reward being the rabbit. It was my reason for attending as many harvesting events as I could. At first the quarry was not spotted in any great number but, as the reaping continued, the area of the crop diminished, as did the rabbits' cover. The odd one or two would make a dash for safety but most would remain within the rapidly weakening security of the corn. At last the remaining standing corn would erupt in an explosion of brown fur and bobbing white tails as the men and children alike set about clubbing as many as possible. The catch would be set aside until the end of harvesting for the day when it would be shared among the victors.

Any barelegged youngster who has spent a day running through the stubble that remains after the binder has cut the corn will know that the lower legs are scratched to the point of bleeding. It was not a problem while you were enjoying the excitement of the hunting, or helping with the stooking. It was later in the evening, after the excitement of the day's adventures had lost its glow, that the pain and soreness became difficult to bear. Mum would always make sure that we were washed and clean before going to our bed. To achieve this she would stand us on the table, then with a large soapy cloth and a bowl of tepid water start the cleaning process. It was at this point that you wished you had never gone anywhere near the cornfield. The strong soap and chafing cloth would bring tears to my eyes, as the open scratches soaked up the carbolic mixture. I accept that there is always a price to pay for enjoyment and I still firmly believe that the gain was worth the pain; however, it shed a whole new light on the definition of stubble rash.

The harvest season was always a period, or so it seemed, of a greater acceptance of youngsters by the adults. Men would always have a cheery greeting for the boys as they arrived in the cornfield. Gentle ribbing and practical jokes were the norm. I became the butt of many of these; being young and in awe of adults, I made an easy target. I remember spending most of one day standing at the side of the field with my rabbit club held high above my head. One of the men had told me that I would give the horse a reference point. If I moved, the horse would wander aimlessly through the cornfield causing havoc with the reaping. They would tease me mercilessly about anything and everything, reducing me almost to tears with frustration. They never tired of the game throughout the whole harvest period, yet once the harvest was gathered in their attitude reverted to the former adult-child relationship.

The harvest was the focal point of the year to the village community. Even though the sire and serf days were not as evident as they once were, the villager's position was still dependent on a successful village economy. This economy was based on the quality of the harvest. If the squire had a good financial year, so then did his workers.

Dad worked as many hours as he possibly could to provide for

Hazelnuts and Moorhens' Eggs

his family, with the exception of Sundays. On this day he worked in the garden and carried out the general maintenance chores that Mum could not manage. We, the children, were sent to Sunday school with our attendance books. The stamp that was placed in the book was proof for Mum and Dad that we had actually been to the church, or so we thought. It was quite a few years later when I realised that Sunday afternoon was 'quality time' for parents. Living as we did in a small cottage with no privacy must have been very restricting; Sunday afternoon, with a guarantee that the children would attend Sunday school, was therefore designated prime time for parents. I would have remained ignorant of this fact had I not fallen into the canal while fishing. We had moved to Pewsey by this time and there obligatory Sunday school was not enforced. I ran all the way home, absolutely soaking wet, to find the doors locked and apparently no one at home. The curtains of my parents' bedroom were drawn. After much wailing by my bedraggled self, Dad appeared. He deigned to let me in but his attitude was far from welcoming. It was very inconsiderate of me to fall into a freezing cold canal on a Sunday afternoon. This was the beginning of a realisation that parents are not there just for the children, and I remember looking at them in a different way from then on.

However, the Manningford Sunday afternoon regime that kept us out of the house had its own reward. After Sunday tea we all changed into our best clothes for the Sunday evening family walk.

This was a ritual that most families performed. A family resembled a brood of ducks, all in single file waddling along the lane. Dad, in the role of the drake, would take the lead followed by the ducklings with the mother duck, Mum, bringing up the rear. Most of the villagers could be seen on these ritual walks and polite greetings were exchanged whenever paths crossed. It didn't matter which route Dad took for the chosen walk, we always, as did the other participants, ended up at the Green Dragon, the only pub in the village. This was the highlight of the week for me. Dad would go inside while Mum and my brother and I would sit on the benches provided at the front in the beer garden. As the families gathered, the fathers would all enter the pub, returning with a shandy for their wives and lemonade for the offspring. The men never stayed outside. That was the women's role, watching over their brood of ducklings until it was time for the return walk. It must have been the afternoon 'quality time' that made Dad so amiable. I was happy with the lemonade. Sunday school had its attractions, the short cut across the streams and meadows being ample reward for me, so everyone was a winner.

The culmination of the Sunday evening walk at the pub provided the ideal opportunity for the villagers to catch up on the happenings in and around the locality. It was also here that most of the ration book coupons were bartered for. One family's needs might be different from another's and negotiated exchanges would take place in the Green Dragon beer garden. This was the realm of the women. The children by now, their lemonade consumed, would find plenty of exciting things to do in the publican's outhouses, of which there were many. Unfortunately the outhouses had held pigs and other livestock in the past and were not the most desirable play areas for a youngster who was wearing Sunday best clothes.

If there was a good harvest, plenty of happy Sundays at the Green Dragon would follow.

It was about a year after Dad was demobbed when he announced that we were going to have a little brother or sister. I have often noted in later life that a person born in 1940 will usually have a brother or sister six years their junior, which is not surprising in the circumstances. It seemed that a child was conceived in case the husband did not return from war, and a child was conceived because he did. The announcement meant nothing to me. He could have told us to expect a new ferret and that would have been acceptable, you can use a ferret, but what use would we have for a baby?

My sister entered the world in February '46 and my brother and I were taken to Mum's bedroom to be introduced to the new arrival. I took one look and said, 'Take her back; she's got a funny face.' I was never allowed to forget that brief welcoming speech.

There was an incident when she was about ten months old that resurrected my record of sibling abuse. There followed a prime example of my complete disregard of health and safety in

Hazelnuts and Moorhens' Eggs

the home, and very little working knowledge of safety awareness.

I shared a large double bed with my brother. This bed was placed against the outer wall of the cottage, the room being too small to allow access to both sides of the bed. A small window, which overlooked the chicken pen and woodpile to the rear of the cottage, was at the same level as the bed. This window, to my knowledge, had never been opened. It had defied all of the attempts by my brother and me to open it in the past. On this particular day Mum had allowed us to take the baby upstairs to play on our bed. I was bouncing her up and down on the mattress and everything was fine. We were having a great time; she was chuckling and gurgling, a perfect example of siblings enjoying the company of one another. As children inevitably do, I became more enthusiastic with the bouncing. Unfortunately I lost control and she bounced against the window.

In a flash she was gone. This was one time when I would have loved to be the one left holding the baby. Why was it always my actions that made our playtimes so ill-fated? Why did I appear destined to endanger my siblings? Why would a window that in the past had proved impervious to opening, suddenly work so efficiently? My brother stared at me in disbelief. I think on this occasion his concern for our sister outweighed his urge to tell Mum that it was my fault.

Our screaming alerted Mum and Mudder but only Mudder had the courage to go around to the rear of the cottage (Mum was too afraid of what she might find). Fortunately, the one who had looked over me on so many occasions did the same for my sister that day. Mudder found her crying quite lustily on a roll of chicken wire in the pen among the hens. She was quickly reunited with Mum who, for some reason, insisted that we be sworn to secrecy – Dad was never to find out about the incident.

There were other occasions when Dad was kept completely in the dark about happenings in our lives; this was always at the instigation of Mum. I remember one such occasion, a few years later, when I wanted to join the Royal Navy as a boy seaman. Mum told me to wait until Dad had left for work, then make my way to Salisbury to the recruiting centre. Did she think he wouldn't notice that his son had disappeared? As it was necessary for him to give written permission to allow me to go, the secret was blown before it became established. My father was not an ogre but there were times when Mum thought that some things were better kept from his attention. As far as I am aware he was never told of my sister's 'maiden flight'. However, on my return from the recruiting office, after my secret signing-on mission, Mum gently informed him of my intentions. At least half of her plan of secrecy had worked and he was completely happy with the outcome.

Pastures Greener?

We were approaching the time for a move from Manningford and the cottage that had been the source of so many happy memories for me. Space was at a premium with the addition of a daughter/sister. Quite a large housing development plan was taking place in the small market town of Pewsey. Council houses were being built and many families from the surrounding villages were being rehoused. This was the direction my parents wanted to take and, although it was a massive step forward for them, it was a massive step backward for me. I loved the cosy comfort of our little cottage, the oil lamps and black lead range, the tin bath carried in from the outhouse once a week, the evenings spent in front of the range shelling hazelnuts with a penknife. No nutcrackers for us – just scrape the pointed end of the nut with the blade of the knife until the join is visible, then insert the point and twist. A whole kernel every time. I would miss Mum heating up her flat irons on the shelf of the range and attacking piles of laundry. The council house might have light at the flick of a switch and hot or cold water at the turn of the tap but it was not going to equal my home here in the village.

Inevitably the allocation of a council house became a reality and Mum and Dad were ecstatic – this was their dream. Pewsey was only two miles away but I was dreading the move. No one would know me and I would know no one. All my friends were here in the village and all the places that made up my adventure park would be lost to me. My dad realised that a lot of his nefarious activities would have to end so he was returning to his trade as a baker. Before conscription he had worked in a bakery in Pewsey. The time had come to resume that employment. Leaving a council estate carrying guns, ferrets, gin traps and snares would be more difficult than stepping from the solitude of the cottage.

A new era was about to begin and I was not at all happy about it. On the day of the move I was instructed to stay with Mudder, possibly for the last time.

Mum and Dad were going to the new home to prepare everything; they would collect me in the evening when all would be ready. I believe Mudder knew how I was feeling about the move because she lavished cuddles and hugs on me throughout the day. The fact that I was encouraged to call her Mudder (my second mum) was proof enough that I was her favourite.

It was quite late in the day when Dad finally came for me. It was time to leave. Joe ran off and refused to say goodbye to me. Our partnership was dissolved for ever! For many years after our move to Pewsey I would walk back to the village to visit Mudder.

The new home was, by our standards, massive. There was a bathroom, so no more carrying the tin bath into the house. We had two flushing toilets; no more the distasteful task for Dad of burying the contents of the dunnock in the garden. Electricity produced light at the flick of a switch and Mum had a cooker, so there would be no more polishing the black lead range. There was an outhouse with an electric copper. As the copper was freestanding there was nowhere to hide from Mum's retribution. The view from every window in the house overlooked other dwellings. There were people everywhere and each one was a stranger.

Mum had wasted no time on the education front and the following morning my brother and I were marched to school. We did not attend the same school because of our age difference and I was left at the infants' school. Within hours I had made friends, discovered that the school straddled the river Avon (ideal for the obligatory wet feet), and that there were many boys in the same predicament as myself.

Dad's place of work, the bakery, was opposite the infants' school so we often walked home at lunchtimes together, Dad carrying a piping hot lardy cake (his speciality) and a hot crusty loaf of freshly baked bread, with me trotting at his side.

This was the beginning of a new life, and not the end of an old one, as I had first feared. Perhaps moving to a town would have some consolation; I was, after all, still within walking distance of

Hazelnuts and Moorhens' Eggs

the canal, and the council estate, with its many ongoing building sites, should provide plenty of adventures. Instead of trees to climb there was scaffolding, and there was a labyrinth of half-built rooms and passageways that could feature as a multitude of useful backdrops. The future looked very promising indeed.

The town boasted a cinema, or picture house as it was known. This was a magnificent source of ideas for us to incorporate into our playtime activities. What appeared on the screen quickly reappeared in the play areas of Pewsey. A sizeable piece of hazelwood would provide a young Robin Hood with a very good bow while the smaller pieces made excellent arrows. A similar piece of the same wood, threaded through a pierced cocoa tin lid, provided many a musketeer with a more than passable sword. The cocoa tin lid provided quite efficient protection for the hand of a fiercely swashbuckling Blackbeard or the more artistic fencing of a musketeer. A stubbier piece of hazelwood made a Sten gun or doubled as a rounders club. The empty cocoa tins that gave up their lids for swordplay found use as an early version of the telephone. We would spend hours passing messages via a length of string connected to two tins. The string was passed through the base of one tin and the base of the other. It was held firmly in place by a fairly large knot then stretched to the extreme. As long as the string was taut it was only a matter of speaking into the tin to communicate, and clamping the tin over your ear to receive a reply.

Dad's beeswax block, borrowed from his fishing tackle, was used to wax the string to enhance the reception. Aping the actions of pirates, musketeers and commando divisions was likely to incur slight injuries, and did just that on occasion. The stick/sword thrust into the stomach, or a glancing blow to the arm or hand was commonplace; the clubbing with the Sten gun sometimes loosened teeth and raised large bruises but usually it was taken in good part.

The prisoner-of-war film raised the most cause for concern. Invariably the film included breaking out of the camp and the most usual way was by tunnelling. Youngsters such as we were quick to copy the actions of the escapers and we had an area that was tailor-made for such adventures. On the outskirts of our housing estate was a large piece of waste ground which I believe had been a sewerage site in bygone years. Over the years it had come to resemble the crater of an extinct volcano. The interior of this volcano was perfect for tunnelling and, being young and adventurous, this is what we did. As children of nine and ten years of age we had no knowledge of pit props and the like; we hailed from Wiltshire and not some northern mining community. Undeterred we would tunnel into the soft earth, the tunnel being just big enough to accommodate our bodies. With the aid of a trowel and a National Dried Milk tin to excavate the soil, we converted the site into what could only be described as a warren. We found that if we burrowed horizontally into the sides, but stayed within three feet of the surface, we could sink small shafts to aid the removal of the soil. These shafts started at a point when passing the soil over or under the body became too awkward. With the aid of a length of string tied to the National Dried Milk tin we were able to lower it to the tunneller who would fill it with soil; once it was filled he would give a sharp tug on the line and it would be drawn up through the shaft. Here it would be emptied and returned.

When the tunneller achieved the extent of his reach once again, another shaft was sunk and the process was repeated. Some of the tunnels terminated by breaking through the surface, creating a bolthole exit, while others carried on in a U-shape until they emerged once more on the inside of the crater. There were some instances of collapsed tunnels but fortunately these occurred overnight and mostly after a rainstorm.

We carried on with this dangerous pastime for many months until one day we arrived and found that the whole warren had been staved in. Every tunnel had been filled or made impassable in one way or another. It transpired that one of the fathers had uncovered information regarding the dangerous practice of young POWs operating in the area, apparently trying to escape by digging tunnels. A few fathers mulled over the information in the local Working Men's Club and a safety meeting was held. They decided to take action before an accident occurred. A few of the fathers joined forces and, with the aid of spades and big boots, completely destroyed the site that had taken months of labour to complete. It was a bitter discovery for us, but it really had been only a matter of time before an accident occurred.

Another avenue opened to us due to the demolition of our escape project. It was still related to the wartime exploits of our heroes. If we couldn't go underground then the alternative was to go above ground – in fact we would become aviators. All of the boys who were raised during the war had a great admiration for the pilots and airmen who flew the fighters and bombers that either raced or droned across the skies. The fascination with bailing out of one of these aircraft was always at the forefront of a healthy boy's imagination.

With this in mind one of our number managed to acquire an old sheet. The 'sheet' might have been a tablecloth, but the outcome would have been the same had either been selected. After a few days of foraging for other materials, rope, string and an old belt, we brought together the first tree-launched parachute. We often made a small parachute from an old handkerchief and as this was usually successful we could see no reason why a larger version should not be equally so. We all set about manufacturing the 'chute. First, ropes were attached to each corner of the sheet and drawn together culminating in a large knot. A belt was added as a harness and the 'chute was completed.

We selected a tree wisely, wisely meaning that it was well away from the sight of any interfering adult. Now all that we needed was a volunteer! I remember that this part of the operation took about three days.

Our choice of 'volunteer' was a boy who would, had it been today, have a nickname such as 'Gullible' or even 'Death Wish'. As it happened his name was Bob. The rest of us were eager to see our 'chute in action and we set about convincing Bob that it would be easy. We claimed that other boys had done it and that he would be the hero of the hour if he would only climb the tree and jump. The cajoling continued for a couple of days. There were even boys who vowed that they had often done it themselves back in the village that they had moved from. I think we just wore Bob down so much that he reluctantly agreed to comply with our wishes. With the belt around his waist and the 'chute over his shoulder he laboriously climbed the tree. Once he was in position we had to start cajoling him all over again as it seemed he was losing his nerve. Eventually Bob was ready to jump and, encouraged by our cheers, he launched himself into space. It had taken almost a week to reach this crucial point only for it to be all over in a second.

If the 'chute had opened it might have lasted three seconds.

We assumed there had been a design fault and that was the reason that Bob was now screaming in agony on the ground.

We gathered around the crumpled form of the failed parachutist who was now sobbing and clutching his ankle with both hands. His father was the local barber and I believed that if word of our participation in the injury to his son reached him, he would seek us out with a cut-throat razor.

My fears were soon allayed when I noticed that Bob had managed to stand unaided and was gingerly trying to take his weight on the suspect ankle. As the pain abated his confidence returned. A new Bob had replaced the old Bob; this was Mark II.

He was soon strutting among us as though he had achieved some kind of hero status. His elevation in the pecking order of our little gang had been worth the suffering that he had endured. If the tunnels had collapsed on him he would have had no status at all. The outcome for any of us would have been disastrous and the actions of the fathers concerned were timely and correct, although it did not seem that way to us at the time.

The surrounding hills forming the Vale of Pewsey were ideal for both winter and summer sledging. At the first fall of snow we would collect as many timber offcuts and useful pieces of wood that could be found and then, with the use of Dad's tools, build a serviceable sledge. It didn't have to be a sleek, attractive model. All that it was required to do was carry one or two boys down the hill without falling to pieces. If we could find strips of metal to tack to the runners it doubled the speed. Where there is grassland and cattle so there is barbed-wire fencing. Our sledges were designed for speed; they did not incorporate a braking system. The safest way to avoid being impaled by barbed wire was to roll from the sledge before reaching the fence.

The fence always seemed to approach at an alarming speed so the timing of abandonment had to be perfect. I have mentioned

Hazelnuts and Moorhens' Eggs

that we were not blessed with long trousers (no concessions were made, even in winter) so after we had rolled from the sledge our downhill momentum was arrested by bare legs, short trousers and freezing snow.

The snow quickly found its way up our trouser legs, invading parts that should never be submitted to that kind of abuse. Finally the crisp rye grass brought us to a halt.

The stubble rash encountered during the harvesting period was nothing compared with the soreness of sledge legs. Stubble rash affected the shins and lower legs, an area of hardy, well-exposed skin, while sledge legs always affected the pale soft area of the upper thighs and usually incorporated the lower buttocks. Luckily the snow thawed and disappeared more quickly than the harvest season lasted. We did have a summer season sledging period which, although less painful, was a much more dangerous pastime. We found that a sheet of galvanised corrugated steel, with the front bent up, was a great substitute for a sledge. The barbed wire was still a hazard but this form of sledging had the added danger of decapitation. We did not realise quite how hazardous this was at the time. Imagine, if you will, two or three boys hurtling down a Wiltshire hillside on a sheet of steel; add a built-in guillotine to the design (bend the front up and over until it faces the rider) and you will appreciate the foolishness of this practice. It did not end in a disaster, which was due more to good luck than sound judgement, and in later years large sheets of cardboard replaced the steel, much less dangerous and equally effective.

Not every part of my childhood was one long, happy-go-lucky catalogue of enjoyment. I experienced a year of what today might be termed a depression: a depression that was brought about by the Eleven Plus.

I was aware of the exam long before I was due to take it. I also knew that if successful I would have to leave all or many of my friends, and carry on my education at Marlborough Grammar School. It was regarded as a very prestigious achievement to win a placement and the pressure started long before you were due to take the exam. I made it known to both of my parents that I had no desire whatsoever to become a member of the grammar school. My brother had been a pupil there for two years and I had seen the change in him. There was also the strain on resources for Mum and Dad. After listening to my protestations they both agreed that I would not have to go. However, there is always a price to pay and they both insisted that I must try my best to pass the exam. The reason for this stipulation was that most of the boys who failed maintained that, because they did not want to go to Marlborough, they had flunked the paper on purpose. Unfortunately many of the parents, through family loyalty, insisted that their offspring had thrown the exam for that reason. There was no way that my parents would be part of a blatant untruth, and told me that, 'Pass or fail son, you must stand by the result, with no fabrications.' It was left that I would not have to go to Marlborough. I believe that it was a relief, financially, to my parents. My brother was enough of a problem to fund and if I were added to the equation it would make matters worse.

The time came for the exam and I passed with flying colours. Thank goodness it was all over at last. I resumed my carefree existence, happily informing anyone who asked of my results. Mum and Dad also told family and friends of my success, happy that I had decided that I did not want to attend the grammar school. Mum scraped together enough money to buy me a grey 'lumber jacket suit' ready for my return to Pewsey Council Mixed School as it was known, after the school holidays.

Somehow my parents, and their honesty, reaped the wrong benefits when the well-meaning, but misguided family and close friends started to exert pressure upon them. 'It is unthinkable that a boy could be allowed to throw away the chance of a lifetime, he must go to grammar school' – and – 'It is a parent's duty to send a boy to Marlborough, no matter what hardship it incurs'. The pressure was quite intense and continued until my wishes were cast aside. I was duly sent for an interview with the headmaster of Marlborough Grammar. This would have been my last chance to avoid becoming a pupil, but I was either too slow or still obeying my parents' last command. Naively, I made the right impression and gave all the right answers and was duly accepted, starting when the school reopened in about three weeks.

The gloom descended as Mum and I travelled back to Pewsey

on the service bus. I would soon learn to hate this Wilts and Dorset double-decker, as it was to be my means of transport to and from school for the next year.

My depression was equal to the gloom that settled on Mum. For all of the insistence by family and friends that I must be given the opportunity to benefit from the education the grammar school would afford, no help was forthcoming from any of them. I tried to portray an attitude that nothing was worth her spending good money on; this in itself was detrimental to my sense of belonging once I had started the first term. The school uniform was a formal grey suit, with the school crest on the breast pocket, and a maroon cap and school tie, depicting the set you were allocated to. My lumber jacket suit, although grey, did not conform to the regulations. A neighbour, whose son was leaving the grammar school, gave my mother his cap and tie. This was gratefully accepted but it meant that I would arrive at school already assigned to C set.

The tie, being maroon with blue stripes, denoted that the wearer was a member of C set. A set was yellow, B set was green and each set was allocated when the pupil joined. The tie would then be bought at the time of allocation. I remember the strange looks that I received, as it appeared I had chosen my own set. The whole ensemble was completed with the trendy addition of an ex-army respiratory bag as a satchel, formerly used as a fishing tackle bag by Dad. Nothing was said, however, and I remained a member of C set for the duration of my time at Marlborough.

I was never singled out by the other pupils for my appearance, I was never bullied and I cannot remember a single disparaging remark. In fact the only embarrassment came from the actions of a couple of teachers.

I had been at school for a few weeks when it became apparent that the cost of school dinners was proving too much for Mum. So, in an effort to make things a little easier, I pretended that I would rather take sandwiches. I said that the food was awful and the portions were too small. A sigh of relief from Mum and I was sent off to school with sandwiches packed in the multi-purpose Oxo tin that she obtained from the Co-op.

Each lunch hour I would wander around the playground,

happily munching my sandwiches, while the rest of the pupils enjoyed their fare in the dining hall. This arrangement lasted about two weeks until a teacher, one of the lunchtime overseers, decided that I should eat in the dining hall with the rest of the pupils. This I grudgingly did, taking great care to conceal my utility lunch box in my respirator bag on my knees beneath the table. After a few days the same teacher demanded that I should be issued with a plate and that my food was to be eaten from the plate in a civilised manner. By this time I began to feel that I was being victimised.

This was the beginning of the end for me. I did not mind the lumber-jacket suit, the second-hand cap and tie, or even the respirator bag, but having to display Mum's sandwiches for all to see was going too far. I have explained that sandwich finesse was not one of my mother's skills. To be fair, as my Dad was a baker, the bread was always soft and fresh in our house and I have learnt in later years just how difficult it is to slice a freshly baked loaf. To maintain a degree of uniformity is almost impossible. Sliced bread was still a long way into the future.

I did as I was instructed but that was the start of my lack of interest in everything pertaining to Marlborough Grammar School. The surprising outcome of my sandwich embarrassment was that, after a few days, another pupil arrived with sandwiches and within a couple of weeks there were enough of us to have a table of our own allocated.

Despite this demonstration of support I still wanted to get away from Marlborough. It began to show in my schoolwork and demeanour. The obligatory homework I completed on the top deck of the bus on my journey home. It resembled the scribble a spider would leave had it fallen into an inkwell. As soon as the bus arrived in Pewsey I would search for my friends, but the barrier between us was evident in their attitude toward me. I was almost treated as leper by them; I was no longer one of the gang.

My parents were aware of the personality change that I was undergoing and realised that this was affecting my way of life. What price education if it meant another five years of misery for me? Dad arranged an interview with the headmaster and after two or three meetings and a review of my school report (dreadful) I was released at parents' request. I suspect the headmaster was glad to be rid of me. I had brought about a few changes that were not in keeping with the traditions of the establishment.

In the history of Marlborough, I was the first pupil to disregard the uniform policy.

I was the first to introduce sandwiches as an alternative to the school dinner, creating a new table arrangement in the hallowed hall of dining.

I also had the notoriety of being the only pupil to be marked present, even though absent, on Wednesday mornings; I deliberately missed the bus as the first lesson was maths and the teacher knew that I would arrive when the lesson was over!

It was akin to being reborn on my return to Pewsey Council Mixed; even the teachers greeted me as a long-lost son. It soon became apparent that I was behind my colleagues in many subjects. I could speak a few sentences in French but in other areas I was sadly lacking. It became a common jibe by my teachers that I must have left my brain at Marlborough. With the feeling of well-being from being back, I soon caught up with the rest and continued my secondary education. It is amazing what can be achieved when a child is happy in his or her surroundings. Mum and Dad were also relieved at my return to the happy-go-lucky child that they had always known.

Schooldays became as enjoyable as any other activity for me, and to be able to pop home during the lunch break for dinner with Mum was a welcome return to normality. The size of her sandwiches never changed but I swear her heart grew bigger. She was probably more pleased than me to have her boy back. I think she felt a little ashamed that she had been pressured into making me do something that she had agreed I would not have to. The family and friends, who had been responsible for the pressure, were strangely silent when my release was confirmed. They too had witnessed the change in me during the year that I had spent at Marlborough. They were also wary of my mother's fiery temperament and sensibly held their silence.

The family photo taken for the Rod's father to carry with him during his service in the Royal Marines in World War II. Rod is sitting on his mother's knee.

The 'tin garage' at the top of the garden. It was from this vantage point that the proprietor spotted the thatch fire and dashed to the rescue with his trusty stirrup pump.

Manningford Abbots Church, the venue of Sunday school meetings. Now deserted and desolate, some headstones remain among the undergrowth, including the one marking Rod's grandparents' grave.

PLEASE DO NOT INJURE

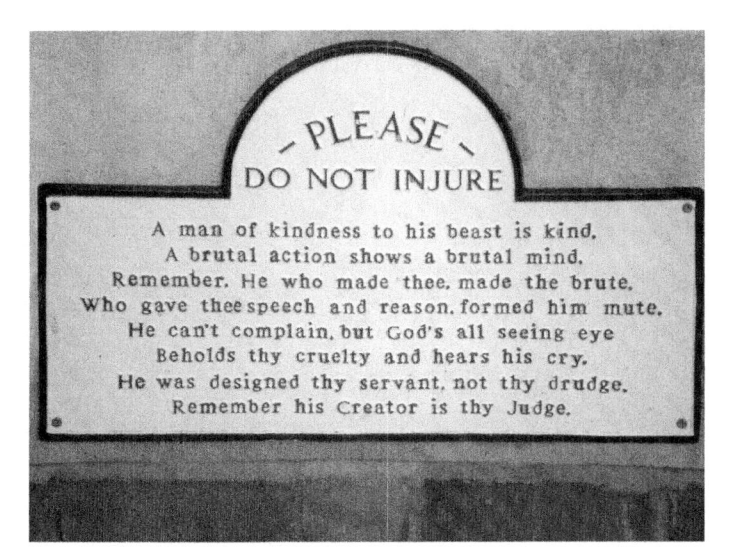

A man of kindness to his beast is kind,
A brutal action shows a brutal mind.
Remember, He who made thee, made the brute,
Who gave thee speech and reason, formed him mute.
He can't complain, but God's all seeing eye
Beholds thy cruelty and hears his cry.
He was designed thy servant, not thy drudge.
Remember his Creator is thy Judge.

The latter-day replacement plaque bearing the poem dedicated to the welfare of the beast of burden that was positioned above the drinking trough at Gashouse Brow.

The original was emblazoned on an ornamental wooden board – it was more pleasing to the eye. However, the message is preserved and remains the same.

*The infant school that Rod attended on relocating to Pewsey.
His mother left him here, a little friendless stranger – by luchtime he had discovered
a multitude of new mischief-seeking companions. Such were the joys of childhood.
The road sign pointing towards Marlborough was not a directive for the pupils to
aspire to reaching Marlborough School!*

*King Alfred gazes down from his pedestal in the centre of Pewsey.
In Rod's youth the thanksgiving service was held here on the last Sunday evening
following the Pewsey Feast/Carnival.*

The Pewsey Vale White Horse.
Subject to appendage enhancement by the village boys from time to time.

The mill race. In Rod's youth the mill wheel was in place (the new brickwork depicts its original position on the mill wall). Upstream from this position was the freshwater swimming hole, Three Bridges.

The tunnel beneath the railway embankment where Rod first encountered the wriggling lamprey colony. These little eel-like creatures prevented him from learning the art of trout tickling.

Normal Service Resumed

The hills that formed the vale were riddled with rabbits and my earlier training with Dad stood me in good stead to catch them. Not to mention a hardware store in the town that offered a very extensive range of wire snares, gin traps, catapult elastic and fishing tackle.

I soon became proficient at supplying Mum with fare for the table. The blackbird incident would never be forgotten, but a rabbit was always acceptable. It was hunter-gatherer foraging that brought us, my friends and me, into an area on the hillside where the chalk 'etching' of the Pewsey White Horse is displayed in all its glory.

There are many notable monuments etched into the chalk hills of Wiltshire. As landmarks they are quite majestic but give no indication of their size when viewed from a distance.

When you go to visit the site of the White Horse it appears as a huge area of chalk with no immediate discernable shape or form. As we approached the fence that enclosed the White Horse an idea started to form in my constantly mischief-activated mind. It was depicted as neither mare nor stallion and I proposed to my companions that, with the aid of our penknives and fingers, we could rectify this. The White Horse was about to become the Rampant White Stallion.

Our first attempt proved to be a failure; it would take more than penknives and fingers to remove the topsoil, so we abandoned the project until we were better equipped. It didn't take long to spread the word among other youngsters that we were about to change the appearance of Pewsey Vale's famous landmark. We clandestinely gathered enough boys together, with an assortment of tools deemed necessary to complete the job, and set off.

It was a well-executed and eye-catching operation. Our idea of equestrian dimensions appears to have been an exaggerated one,

Hazelnuts and Moorhens' Eggs

as when viewed from the A345, it proved to be the most well-endowed stallion ever seen on the hills. It was a short-lived liberation for the stallion; within a week it was gelded and returned to its former asexual state.

The local scout troop was given the responsibility of maintaining the White Horse site from that time on. They undertook the weeding, cleaning and removal or obliteration of any added appendages that might appear on the site. I cannot remember any other incident of cosmetic enhancement to other White Horses in the area, so our notoriety must have been short-lived. It was never our intention to become notorious through our escapades and I cannot remember any urge, or yearning, to be recognised for our pranks. We were certainly not bored so it could not have been a cry for attention, as so many acts of vandalism are labelled today.

My mischievous escapades became seriously curtailed by the need to help Dad with his efforts to keep a roof over our heads. Although he was employed as a baker the wage was not enough to support three children and my father would not allow a wife of his to work, other than assist him with the garden (a mother's place was in the home). He worked in the bakehouse from seven o'clock in the morning until noon, then, after a quick lunch at home, he made his way to the local cemetery. There he would don the cap of caretaker and gravedigger until five o'clock. Then he would return home for tea and a brief rest before going back to the bakehouse to prepare the dough for the following day. I remember him returning home every evening at nine o'clock. There was no bread on Sundays so Saturday night was his free period when he would go to the Working Men's Club for a well-earned stout.

My brother and I would lie awake in our bedroom waiting excitedly for his return. Within minutes he would summon us to come down and collect the bottle of Vimto that he always brought home for us; this routine became a ritual.

As children, we were expected to work with him in the local cemetery. The grass cutting was Dad's domain and path weeding was for his boys. Even this workload was not rewarding enough, so he decided to keep a few pigs to bring in extra cash. This also became Dad's boys' responsibility. My brother and I were given the chore of collecting potato peelings and vegetable waste from participating neighbours. Their reward was a very desirable joint of fresh pork when the pigs were ready for market. Dad always had one pig slaughtered for our own use. I never had the desire to eat the chitterlings after seeing them turned inside out with the aid of the copper stick. Even the final presentation, snow white and plaited, did nothing to tempt me into trying them. To this day I have never tasted chitterlings. The taste of home-cured bacon, however, will stay in my memory for ever.

The pigs were kept a considerable distance, approximately half a mile, from our house in sties rented from a local pub landlord. Everything pertaining to the pigs' well-being had to be transported by hand. Dad would boil the collected scraps in Mum's electric copper, then have us carry it in the old tin bath (the same bath that we once used to bathe in), to the pigsties. The contents were stowed in two large wooden barrels until, at scheduled feeding times, meal would be added and the resulting mixture was then fed to the pigs. The peelings were collected twice a week; the pigs were fed twice a day. They were mucked out once a week with most of this work being undertaken by my brother and me. The dung was kept at the site until it had matured enough to be used as manure.

I became aware of how ergonomically unfriendly Dad's planning was. The peelings were collected all over our estate (by Dad's boys). Preparation was done at the house and then carried to the pigs (by Dad's boys). It was consumed, digested and passed through the pigs, to be mucked out and stacked (by Dad's boys).

Once the resulting dung became manure it was wheelbarrowed to his allotment, a back-breaking distance (by Dad's boys).

The allotment was as distant geometrically, in the opposite direction from the house, as the pigs were in the other. The raw material, from peelings to manure, must have travelled miles before being laid to rest beneath the fertile soil of Dad's allotment. The allotment was also tended, in the main, by Dad's boys!

The pattern of chores was mainly seasonal but, when a boy reached the age of thirteen and the school holidays (a summer break of six weeks) came around, then he was expected to find

Hazelnuts and Moorhens' Eggs

gainful employment on local farms and nurseries. In many cases during harvesting, a boy would be taught the rudiments of driving a tractor, thereby releasing an adult farm worker to perform the heavier work in the field. I remember it did not entail changing gear, just releasing the clutch and creeping along as the men loaded the trailer. I had a favourite farm where I would often spend school breaks; it was smaller than most of the farms in our area but it had more to offer a boy. There were only three farm labourers employed at Buckleaze Farm. It was more a smallholding than a farm but it allowed me more scope than the larger arable farms, which concentrated on crops more than livestock. I was allowed to milk one particular cow. Unbeknown to me at the time was that this was the most unproductive cow in the entire herd and the men wanted nothing to do with her. I was quite happy to struggle on with the process, believing that I was doing a fine job. The cow became almost a pet to me and the farmer, who often helped with the milking, shared the amusement of his farmhands when I proudly produced the meagre contribution, hardly enough to serve with the average helping of cereals.

The farm also boasted a beautiful shire horse and, although it was not gainfully employed on a full-time basis, it was brought out when the potato harvest was due. The farmer always managed the horse and I believe it was more a family friend than a beast of burden. It was wonderful to see this old horse pulling a single-shear plough along the raised potato rows and the golden tubers being unearthed for the pickers to gather. The potatoes could have been harvested by mechanical means but I think it was as much an act of nostalgia for the farmer as for the horse; it gave the horse a reason for being, and the farmer justification for keeping an old friend in retirement.

I was allowed to groom the old horse and reward it with locust beans, much to the amusement of the three old farmhands. The stable was quite narrow and the horse was always tethered close to the stable wall. One of the hazards of grooming became evident when getting between the horse and the wall. The men, from experience, knew when to move quickly but to ensure their entertainment they failed to tell me of a quirk that the old horse had. Without any warning it would lean on you, pinning you against the stable wall. It did not exert any great pressure but it was enough to keep you immobile for as long as it wished. When it first happened to me I thought my time had come. The more I struggled the more it leaned on me and it was my yells of fright that made the old farmhands finally relax and give it some locust beans. Once it had the beans it eased the pressure and allowed me to wriggle free. Evidently it was the old horse's party piece and any newcomer to the farm was eventually subjected to it, much to the amusement of the farmhands.

Their sense of humour took some strange turns throughout the time that I spent with them. I was often dispatched across the fields with a sickle and crooked stick to cut down thistles; it stopped the spread of seeds. One day we were all walking together, the men had scythes and we were about to spread out and clear the area of thistles. Suddenly one of them yelled and jabbed the head of his scythe into the long grass. I was interested to see what it was that had caught his attention. Maybe he had pinned a rabbit down? Unfortunately for me it was a grass snake, and as I remember quite a large one. Whooping and hollering, one of the men grabbed the snake while the other grabbed me. Then, pulling my shirt collar from the back, he proceeded to drop the snake down the opening. My next memory was of three very worried faces peering down at me where I had collapsed, fainting in sheer terror.

Not all the pranks played were as terrifying as the snake episode and the men were extremely sorry that they had put me through such an ordeal. I continued to work there in my spare time until it was time to finish my schooling, and I have to say that I enjoyed every minute.

There were many chores that child farm labourers were engaged in and the money earned was a help to both Mum and us. I have mentioned that country boys did not obtain long trousers until quite late into their teens. This farm work provided the means for us to buy our own. Returning to school after the summer holidays wearing a pair of grey flannel 'long 'uns' was worth every minute of time spent picking potatoes or gathering bales of straw. I believe that, had I not gone to work and bought

Hazelnuts and Moorhens' Eggs

my own flannels, I would have finished my schooldays in shorts. Long trousers were another rite of passage.

The completion of the gathering of the harvest is celebrated by a week of festivities, Pewsey Carnival, or as it is known to older members of the community, Pewsey Feast. It always attracted large crowds in my youth and was the highlight of the year for us. The town was decorated with lights and banners throughout. The river Avon, where it ran through the town, was criss-crossed with suspended fairy lights, which were lit with fresh candles every night. This always created a breathtaking spectacle. A ducking stool was set up on the riverside and volunteers were requested to risk the chance of immersion in cold water. Two funfairs arrived every year, a week before the main attraction, this being the carnival procession. The local people decorated the floats and tractors with themes of their choice and the illuminated procession would take a designated route through the town and around the outskirts. The procession was open to all and prizes were awarded for the best entry. I have known the streets of Pewsey to be so crowded that you could not choose a direction to take; you were literally carried along in the crush.

The culmination of the week's celebrations was a thanksgiving service held on the Sunday evening in the marketplace under the stony gaze of King Alfred, whose statue stands in the centre of the town. The procession was the main attraction of the week and many people from surrounding villages flocked into the town to enjoy the spectacle. There was one year during my later teens when the procession was cancelled because of an outbreak of foot-and-mouth disease. Although the farm vehicles were barred, a few stalwarts managed a foot procession. Information reaching me in my adopted county of Norfolk today leads me to believe that the Health and Safety Executive are achieving what foot-and-mouth failed to do. Progress is a wonderful thing!

The origins of the feast, and its reasons for being, have probably been forgotten by many and unknown by many more. To my friends and me it was the culmination of a long spell of hard work and a means to an end, the end in my case being help for Mum financially.

My reward was the beginning of a wardrobe of my own, in

which grey flannels played a prominent part. The days of scabbed knees and nettle rash were hopefully a thing of the past.

During my recreation periods (between weeding paths and feeding pigs) I loved to walk to the canal and fish. Fishing became a favourite pastime of mine as I grew older. It would become one of the many contributing factors to the changing attitude between father and son. This was a transition that I failed to recognise until much later in life. I was in my early teens and beginning a period where I would challenge my father, as all boys tend to do without being aware of it. This 'challenging' is nature's way of saying that the time to leave the protection of the nest is approaching. A very common method that a boy will employ when attempting to challenge his father is sitting in Dad's favourite chair when he is out of the room. On the father's return the boy will remain seated until he is given a warning look and evicted by the father applying gentle but firm pressure with the hand to the back of the head; this action is usually accompanied by a low growl or the human equivalent, 'Come on – out'. It doesn't matter how far we try to remove ourselves from the animal world, we all subconsciously retain the basic instincts that nature has provided. Fathers want their sons to do better than themselves; unfortunately, the transition from 'novice' to 'accomplished' can be confrontational. If we could put old heads on young shoulders, or turn back clocks, would we do things differently? It took years for me to understand that the tutoring and preparation my Dad gave me was given in unconditional love, and not something that I should try to better him at in a competitive way. Nature is another mystery that moves in a specific way. By the time we recognise the wisdom of our parents we have become parents ourselves.

On my route to the canal to indulge in my favourite pastime, I often stopped for a while at a place named Gashouse Brow. It was here that an old stone horse trough was sited alongside a tributary to the Avon. Erected above the trough was an ornamental board with a hand-painted verse dedicated to the beast of burden; a meaningful poem that I have retained in my memory to this day. The original horse trough and board have long gone but I believe that the poem has been reinstated on a metal plaque and placed where the hand-painted board stood for so many years. Many of

Hazelnuts and Moorhens' Eggs

my boyhood friends, now in their seventies, will probably remember that poem word for word. Anyone with an affinity to animals would never forget it.

I have traced the poem to *The Ladies' Equestrian Guide*, 1857 – author unknown.

Some sources say that this is an old Shaker poem. The original version refers to 'God's omniscient eye' and not 'all-seeing eye'. I can only assume that when the verse was painted on to the board the word 'omniscient' was considered a little too highbrow for the average Wiltshire drayman, as it most certainly would have been to me!

> A man of kindness to his beast is kind.
> A brutal action shows a brutal mind.
> Remember, He who made thee made the brute,
> Who gave thee speech and reason formed him mute.
> He can't complain, but God's all-seeing eye
> Beholds thy cruelty and hears his cry.
> He was designed thy servant, not thy drudge,
> Remember, his creator is thy judge.

The canal was the point of interest for so many childhood adventures. As I have stated, it was a first-time venue for many activities but the most enjoyable was the fishing. There is something tranquil and satisfying about fishing in the canal. The water is still so there is no need to keep repositioning tackle as you do in running water. The water is dark and mysterious, with so many dark weed-covered patches that a youngster imagines all sorts of denizens lurking in its depths. There is always the chance of a family of swans elegantly paddling along, hissing their disapproval at the young human that has dared to trespass on their domain. We were convinced that a swan could, and would, break your arm with one swipe of its wing. I was terrified that I would not be able to retrieve my fishing tackle before the swan snaffled it from the bottom of the canal and swallowed the hook. We were doubly convinced that the swan would attack if it were leading a family of cygnets. In my experience, the most 'hostile' action I ever recall the swan performing was hissing. This was sometimes accompanied by treading water while flapping its wings. This was more than enough to send a boy scrabbling up the canal bank for safety.

As well as swans there was also the discovery, usually too late, that you had chosen a 'fishing hole' that incorporated a previously undetected wasps' nest; always unwelcome, as was the ants' nest. The midges, which seemed determined to eat you alive, were a nuisance, but for some reason we accepted them as a necessary evil.

The canal was divided into regional sections. Each area, or section, had its own fishing authority and a licence was required to fish that particular stretch. During my youth the canal was never used for the purpose for which it was designed. A horse-drawn barge or any form of water-borne transport was never seen. Fishing was its main use, with swimming and ice skating being the other popular seasonal activities.

It seems that with the advent of time the canal has been reinstated as a waterway that now supports a very busy narrowboat population. The place where we as children could fish, swim and play freely has now become a no-go area for such activities. There are Water Authority rules and regulations that restrict many of the practices that were second nature to us. Canal fishing is more enjoyable, and certainly more productive, if the baited hook is allowed to remain in one position for a reasonable length of time; if you have to persistently reel it in to avoid narrowboats then the object of tranquil fishing is destroyed. A participant in a fishing competition informed me recently that he had counted fifty-seven narrowboats and one Dutch barge passing throughout the duration of the competition. This continual disruption, coupled with the rules of where you can and cannot fish, has all but ended what was once a blissful pastime.

The canal offered so many thrills, some exciting and some frightening. Learning to swim encompassed both categories; there was the excitement of reaching the far side of the lock unaided, albeit with an older boy in attendance, as you frantically dog-paddled the four or five meters that, once mastered, denoted that you were now a competent swimmer. The frightening aspect was perpetuated by the constant sighting of the giant pike that was

Hazelnuts and Moorhens' Eggs

rumoured to patrol that particular stretch of the canal. This pike, according to some boys, was in excess of five feet and often swam alongside them, glaring at them with a glinting evil eye. Needless to say the pike was never caught; it never attacked anyone and for some incredible reason, it had never been seen by anyone over the age of fourteen years! It is fair to say that the Monster of Paine's Bridge existed only in the imagination of the Kennet and Avon young swimmers' association. Unfortunately the imagination can be as daunting as reality when out of one's depth.

The canal was also a great supporter of waterfowl, the moorhen being perhaps the most prolific. Owing to the lack of water-borne traffic, the reeds bordering the canal were allowed to grow in great profusion. This allowed the moorhen plenty of cover for the purpose of nest building. The moorhen builds a nest at the base of a suitable growth of reeds, a raft-like platform that should, or could, be undetectable. As the reeds grow the nest becomes quite well hidden, but for some obscure reason, known only to the moorhen, they bend the top of each reed above the nest to create a cover. I don't believe it is an attempt to form a roof for weather protection, more an attempt to avoid detection. This makes the hunter-gatherer's job so much easier. As boys we would wander along the canal bank on either side and quite easily spot the bent-over reeds. All that remained was to remove our shoes and socks, roll up our trouser legs and wade out to the nest.

In every gathering of youngsters there will always be one who professes to be a fount of knowledge; our little gathering was no different. Our fount, in the guise of a self-styled culinary wizard, convinced the rest of the gang that you could fry an egg on a dock leaf. We had matches, we had combustible material, we had dock leaves and we had moorhens' eggs. Could he prove his theory? We quickly built a small bonfire and, with the aid of some dry grass, produced a very smoky pyre. The dock leaves were laid on top, the theory being that the moisture in the leaf would be sufficient to fry, boil, or poach the eggs. To be fair to our fount, it did work in part. We all agreed at the time that it could be used in extreme emergencies to promote survival. Later that evening, however, in the confines of my bedroom, I was convinced that I needed a different type of aid for my survival! Mum was holding cold compresses to the back of my neck and I was regurgitating the contents of the day's foraging. I was becoming a fount, not of knowledge, but of lessons learnt.

The canal was not the only swimming facility open to us. The river Avon played a part in our aqua-sports. This was to the relief of our parents. Mum did not wholeheartedly agree with my habit of immersing myself in rank canal water. To her it was stagnant. The weeds were also one of her concerns; a child could easily become entangled in them. In many ways she was right, although the weeds should have been the least of her worries as we avoided them like the plague. The monster pike was often spotted lurking near weeds (once again, not by anyone over the age of fourteen), obviously waiting to take a youngster by surprise. The Avon, however, was fresh running water, drinkable, clean and perfectly healthy, until we entered it.

Our favourite spot was about a half mile from Paine's Bridge, our usual canal venue. The river ran through a small bridge that comprised three arches and was therefore referred to colloquially by us as 'Three Bridges'. The river entered the bridge at a right angle and was thus a little slower at this point. It was across these arches that we built our dam. We would gather many large stones from the riverbed. This produced a two-fold advantage, increasing the depth of water and providing material for the dam. We would dam one arch at a time, ensuring that our materials were not carried away. We always left one archway partially clear to avoid impeding the river's passage completely. A very serviceable reservoir would quickly fill and a pool would be created for the enjoyment of all. This process became a summer ritual and adults would sometimes come and join us.

The river meandered on through farmland and down to the disused mill. The mill wheel was in position but I cannot remember ever seeing it turning. From the mill it passed under a lane and on towards the railway embankment. The embankment was very high at this point and a dark mysterious tunnel allowed the river to flow beneath, on its journey towards Pewsey.

The Avon also contained trout, a fine offering to present to Mum, and welcome at any time. I only carried a hand line if I intended foraging for trout. I had watched my father tickle trout when we lived in Manningford, but had never tried doing it myself. I was of the opinion that you could catch fish far easier with a worm, lowered from a bank or river bridge, than you could by standing motionless for an eternity and tickling them. The dark tunnel under the railway embankment, however, prompted me to try Dad's method. A friend and I decided to enter this tunnel one day with the sole intention of practising fish tickling. We were wading quietly along, the water being no higher than our knees, when my attention was drawn to what I thought were young eels, or elvers. My first inclination was to run – I was always nervous of the canal eel. They were far too snake-like for me. The exaggerated stories about them – that you can't kill them, that they will not die until the sun goes down, that they will still wriggle for hours even after their heads are cut off – all fuelled a fear of them in me. Here I was, surrounded by thousands of them, in a gloomy tunnel with bare legs. Luckily my friend of the day held no fear for the little monsters, and very quickly caught a couple in his hand. This was my introduction to the lamprey.

We decided there and then that we must return with jars and capture a few of these fascinating little creatures. I kept my collection of lampreys in Dad's old tin bath, the bath of many roles. At the time it was being used as a live-bait tank for pike bait. I studied my latest acquisition with all the enthusiasm of young piscatorial researcher. They have a sucker in place of a mouth and I believe that they attach themselves to fish. Incorporated in this sucker are rasp-like teeth that they use to feed from the flesh of their host. A past king of England is recorded as having died from eating a surfeit of lampreys. The childhood mine of useless information gained stature with every new venture.

Drier Pursuits

All creatures great and small were studied, sometimes collected and catalogued, or just taken home in the hope that they would become a pet. My favourite was a small hedgehog that I found wandering the hedgerows one day. I was sure that it had been abandoned and therefore would make the perfect pet. I nursed it and provided a box for its comfort. It was active for two whole days. On the third morning in my role as a hedgehog's surrogate parent, my mother woke me with a cup of tea accompanied by the announcement, 'Your hedgehog is dead'. Mum was not an unfeeling person by nature, but sometimes her ability to convey bad news left much to be desired.

My little sister, she of aerobatic fame, had reached an age where she wanted to join me in my activities. Mum thought this was quite natural and insisted that I looked after her whenever I left the house. This was all very well in theory but Mum was not aware of the adventures, some hazardous, some not, that we indulged in. In many ways my sister was a burden that I was forced to bear but it did form a very strong bond between us, a bond that has lasted a lifetime. There were advantages for me in this arrangement. She was the apple of my Dad's eye; she only had to smile at him and he was putty in her hands. This was where being responsible for her paid dividends. The Rex cinema was the centre of entertainment for us, showing three films a week. My sister loved the cinema but was too young to go alone; it was my duty to take her. Dad had never paid for me to go to the cinema in the past, no matter how much I had begged and pleaded, yet when his little 'Tuppence', as he affectionately called her, fluttered her eyelashes, he quickly produced the price of two seats, one shilling and tuppence, every time. I must confess that I used this sibling secret weapon on many occasions.

Our adventures sometimes took us to some very eerie places in the Pewsey Vale, eerie because of the content of some of the areas that we visited. We were usually on egg-collecting missions or just wandering for the fun of it when we would discover a gamekeeper's gallows. This was a place where a farmer, or gamekeeper, displayed kills. The kills would be what were then regarded as pests. There was usually a magpie, crow, hawk, jay and a jackdaw, together with a squirrel and weasel, all suspended by the neck. The list of victims would vary from day to day and from site to site. As children we would stand and stare in fascination at the display of decaying wildlife. It was never clear to me what purpose the gallows served. Perhaps the farmer, or gamekeeper, thought that when other like creatures saw the carnage, they would avoid the area. With latter-day knowledge of what defines a particular bird or animal as a pest, it would seem there were many miscarriages of justice in the animal kingdom in that era. We have advanced quite considerably in our protection of various species since those dark days. The wood pigeon is a prime example of the changing attitude of man towards pests.

I can remember the wood pigeon having a reputation as the most nervous and flighty bird in the countryside. If you entered a field in my childhood, the pigeon was the first bird to take flight. To shoot a pigeon it had to be in flight, as it was virtually impossible to stalk in a hedgerow or tree. The only way to approach the pigeon in a tree was when it was nesting and loath to leaving its eggs or young. Today, sixty years later, I have pigeons walking around my garden, almost treating me with disdain, especially if it is time for their afternoon visit to the birdbath. I visualise two breast fillets per bird, bubbling gently in a casserole, or baking under a salt crust each time they drop in.

I can imagine Dad turning in his grave as I allow them the freedom of the garden. Not only would he be annoyed that I make no attempt to catch them for food but also that I allow them to eat my produce, something certainly unheard of in his day.

If I had been told when I was a boy that wood pigeons would be seen feeding from garden bird tables in years to come, I would have scoffed at the idea. Now every source of food that my dad taught me to hunt all those years ago wanders into my garden. Ducks bring their young, as do pheasants and now I am even host to muntjac deer. Life can be quite difficult for a retired poacher.

Fortunately there is as much, or more enjoyment in studying them as could be gained from popping them into a cooking pot.

Perhaps my dad, had he been alive today, would have had the same outlook. He poached for food as a necessity and although it would appear that he only appreciated nature for what he could gain, he in fact had a great affinity with her. I am sure that he would be a conservation supporter and protector of all wildlife if he were alive today. I know that he would be concerned, as many country folk are, that mankind has interfered with the feeding habits of our garden birds. Peanuts are not indigenous to Great Britain yet we have the majority of our garden birds solely reliant on them. Heaven forbid that there will ever be a global peanut crop failure. Even the woodpecker can be seen visiting peanut feeders, which I feel should be cause for concern. Misguided acts of kindness by man can sometimes do more harm than good. I daresay that we already have a large variety of bird species that would perish if the easily available peanut were to disappear from the bird table. The sight of the blackbird stomping on the lawn and pulling a resisting worm from its hole is far more entertaining than a host of blue tits feeding from a man-made peanut dispenser.

The council refuse site was situated a considerable distance from the town, above the valley on Pewsey Hill. This proved to be a great source of bicycle parts for the local boys. Armed with a selection of spanners, we would set off for the 'dump' to spend the day foraging.

The refuse site was a veritable treasure trove of discarded odds and ends. The most valued by us were the bicycle parts. Wheels, frames and handlebars were all coveted by the dump urchins. After collecting all of the useful spare parts that were available, the process of assembling a machine to ride home on would begin. As long as there was a frame and two wheels we were happy. Sprockets, pedals, tyres and brakes would come later; for the moment, the basics were all that mattered. The term 'recycling' was not in everyday use in those days but this was recycling in the literal sense. The return journey down the valley was by road, the gradient of which, as I remember, was quite frightening.

Not one of us would walk while in possession of Heath Robinson transport. The downhill flight would begin, rapidly gathering momentum as the gradient increased.

The emergency braking system entailed reaching around the front forks with your leg and applying pressure to the rim of the wheel with your foot. I saw smoke, on numerous occasions, pouring from my shoe when the friction became too great. I have no recollection of any injury or harm befalling us, proving to me once again that someone, or something, was always looking over us.

It was during these trips that we noticed the rabbit population beginning to show signs of suffering from the symptoms of myxomatosis. From hunting the rabbit for food with every instrument at our disposal, the gin trap and snare being the most barbaric, we became mercy killers. I can remember feeling genuine pity for the poor little animal.

Myxomatosis reduced them to blind and helpless objects of pity. They would sit in the open, unaware of anything around them, their sightless, mucus-filled eyes and grotesquely swollen heads portraying the symptoms of the disease. It was an act of mercy to dispatch them as humanely as possible. We did this as often as our busy schedules would allow. I remember the fifties when every field and hedgerow was alive with brown fur and bobbing white tails. This sight was rendered a rarity by myxomatosis. The occasional hare sported the only brown fur and bobbing white tail sighted thereafter. The hare was unaffected by the disease but, as my family did not regale it as a favourite dish, it held little interest for me. The gamey-flavoured hare was allowed to run freely, high on the hills with impunity.

The hills were a good place to observe the skylark. We would lie down on our backs in the tall rye grass and gaze up into the sky. Skylarks could be seen hovering at extreme heights. Our plan was to watch the descent of the bird. This it did in stages; eventually dropping into the grass. This was where it would have its nest, or so we believed. The object of the exercise was to procure a skylark's egg for my collection. I cannot remember the number of unsuccessful outings that I made to the hills in search of the elusive egg. I never achieved my aim in that respect. It was a disappointment, but I still retained lead position in the hierarchy of egg collectors by being the only boy with a cuckoo's egg in our gang. The egg had been laid in a hedge sparrow's nest. One would think that the female hedge sparrow would be surprised to discover on her return, not only a much larger egg than her own, but one of a totally different colour. Such is the wonder of nature. It was my one and only sighting of a cuckoo egg throughout many years of egg collecting.

Summation

As I recount the exploits of my friends and myself I become more and more aware of the restrictions placed on the youth of today. When I decided to document the memoirs of my childhood, it was to try to give youngsters an insight into the 'freedom to roam' that was open to my generation. No doubt the present younger generation would argue that it is better to have all the trappings of modern times. How could a wireless that was reliant on power from an 'accumulator' compare with a digital television? Could a wind-up gramophone provide the entertainment that an iPod or MP3 player does today?

The modern-day youth may feel that there is no need to roam when, with one click, they can surf the net and visit the known world from the comfort of their bedroom.

The progress in technology during my lifetime has been mind-boggling. In many ways it has improved everyone's quality of life but in some areas it has caused as much harm as good. The media, being a prime example, enables us to receive news of every fad, fashion or cult-type happening anywhere in the world in seconds. It can also spread alarm faster than a viral infection travels and, as with most viruses, becomes difficult to treat.

Parents have become overprotective – and who can blame them? – while the compensation culture has brought about the overzealous activities of numerous safety bodies who seem determined to deny any youngster the normal 'rite of passage' accidents in life. I was always led to believe that to achieve immunity to a disease you must be exposed, in part, to the cause. I feel that we are creating a generation of hermits who spend their lives in the sanctuary of their bedrooms, communicating only via the Internet. There is a wealth of childhood adventures to be enjoyed and it is a fact that every adventure carries risks.

The trees that were our climbing frames are still there, the streams and fields that were our paddling pools and playgrounds can still provide a youngster with educational and recreational activities. Wildlife has not changed to such a degree that it is no longer interesting to a young and enquiring mind. Progress has made many changes but the wonders of Mother Nature are still in place. Farmers are not ogres – if you open a gate to gain access to a field, be sure to close it behind you. If a field is planted with a crop, walk around the edge. Never disturb or annoy any farm animal and always take any litter away with you. All these disciplines were inherent to country children and because we adhered to them our freedom to roam was limitless. Today there are far less hedgerows to explore or trees to climb, but birds still find places to build their nests and youngsters still have the need to flex their growing bodies; it is all part of growing into a strong and healthy adult. There will always be the rite of passage mishap, but don't be discouraged.

It has always been my belief that when man was created he was given many senses; taste, sight, touch and smell being but a few. Included in nature's magnificent selection of senses is the sense of pain. This is nature's safety-awareness system. From a very early age we become aware that pain, wherever possible, is best avoided; pain is unpleasant. It is nature's way of deterring you from charging headlong into a precarious or dangerous situation. Nature makes you aware that a certain action you are about to embark on could hurt, so you automatically do a risk assessment and proceed with caution.

As you mature, the sense of pain and its consequences become common to you, and because of this you will find that you are blessed with the most important sense of all, 'common sense'. If you acknowledge the warnings when common sense is engaged, then you should proceed through life in reasonable safety.

Childhood is a very important part of the journey through life; unfortunately it appears to be getting shorter with each generation. The urge to reach adulthood has become a race, but it is a competition that one should only take part in with the correct training. Childhood is that training. Every building requires good foundations if it is going to stand the test of time. To achieve the best results each stage of the construction requires the guidance of a surveyor. A building surveyor will not condone any short cuts.

As parents, we are the surveyors of our children's construction and we should not condone or encourage any short cuts from childhood to adulthood.

My life, from foundations through two storeys, attic, roof, and now approaching the fitting of the final chimney pot, has been a journey of three stages: childhood – adulthood – dotage.

Of the three I consider the most important to be the foundations – childhood.

Old Heads and Young Shoulders

When you were young, were you ever told life would be grand when you grew old?
Do you think that they were right?
Did they ever mention the potions and pills, needed to ward off the various ills
That creep up in the night?
Did you believe your joints would creak? Or a cough would leave you feeling weak?
The price of growing old.
My dad would say in his wise old way, 'Son, you'll suffer with "screws" one day.'
'But I guess you'll not be told.'
He did the same things when he was a boy, lots of adventures out there to enjoy:
The wet feet and the water.
Cold canal water to the top of your legs, how else can you gather moorhens' eggs?
Rheumatics will grant no quarter.
On through your youth, knowing no fears, trying to emulate all of your peers,
Going downhill with class.
Listen to reason – what is the point? You're determined to sample a beer and a joint.
Were you really such an ass?
Parents imply it's the wrong way to go; they're only adults, what would they know?
They wouldn't understand.
Now I look back and, I recall, I was a pig-headed brat and a right know-it-all.
I didn't need a hand.
Onward and upward until you're full grown, wife and a mortgage, kids of your own.

You begin to see the light.
Those who loved you, from the day you were born,
    parents you often treated with scorn,
You now realise, were right.
With kids of your own to break your heart, instil in
    their minds, right from the start.
Be a saint, and not a sinner.
Life wasn't designed as an easy path, but try to endure
    all its trials with a laugh.
You will always be a winner,
If you can look back when you're old and grey, and
    with hand on heart, truthfully say,
'I think I've done it right.'
Then despite the aches and memory losses, if you can
    produce more ticks than crosses
You'll be all right on the night.
I'd like to think my time on earth, after God's review,
    shows I've proved my worth.
I'll be content to toddle off.
Life is a process, as with wine and cheeses: the more it
    matures, the better it pleases.
I can hear the youngsters scoff!
So, from this journey, what have I learned? Well,
    nothing is free; it has to be earned,
The reward is a happy life.
An important point I need to stress; my journey
    would only mean emptiness
Without my friend, my wife.

Printed in Great Britain
by Amazon